HUMAN RESOURCE

PRACTICE in AFRICA

A Soft Skills Development
Guide for HR Professionals

Dr. Geneva Musau

HUMAN RESOURCE PRACTICE IN AFRICA

Copyright © 2011, Dr. Geneva Musau

Dr Geneva Musau
Life Coaching Foundation
Nairobi, Kenya.

geneva.musau@yahoo.com
+233–266 000005

ISBN: 978-9988-5262-8

Design
Combert Impressions Ltd, Ghana
Tel: +233-302-240557

Human Resource

Practice in Africa

*A Soft Skill Development Guide
for HR Professionals*

Dr. Geneva Musau

ABOUT THE AUTHOR

Dr Geneva Musau has over 19 years of Corporate work experience and for most of these years as the Head of a Human Resources Function. She has contributed to HR transformation and people development in leading Global and International organisations including *Barclays* (Financial Services), KPMG (Management Consulting), Oxfam GB (Not for Profit), *Zain/Airtel* (Telecommunications) and British American Tobacco (FMCG).

Geneva gained experience from the business side (Supply Chain Management and Export Marketing) prior to joining Human Resource practice. The advantage of having worked in business prior to joining HR is evident in her service orientation and desire to get customer insights before implementing HR initiatives. She has experience leading and working with HR teams in *Kenya, Uganda, Tanzania, Uganda, Rwanda, Burundi, DRC, Ethiopia, Somalia, Eritrea, North Sudan, South Sudan and Ghana.* She brings a unique contribution to the HR agenda due to her broad experience in HR practice from contrasting perspectives: Regional level vs. Country as well as International level vs. Local.

Geneva has a PHD in HR Management from AIU (USA), a Master of Arts in HR Management from Demontfort (UK), a Masters in International Business Administration from USIU-Africa (Kenya) and a Bachelor of Commerce from University of Nairobi (Kenya). She is a certified coach, a member of the Association for Coaching (MAC UK) and a valued mentor to many HR practitioners. She serves as a member of the Ashesi (Premier University in Ghana) Corporate Council.

She is the author of a Personal Development book, The Lost Laws of Success. Details of this book can be accessed at *www.thelostlawsofsuccess.com*. She is also the CEO of a foundation, Life Coaching Foundation, which supports needy girls with bursary and tuition support. Additional information on the foundation can be viewed at *www.lcfkenya.org*.

If you would like to get in touch with the author, please write to *geneva.musau@yahoo.com*

CONTENTS

vi

Acknowledgements

I am really indebted to many people that have made this project possible. It is impossible to name everyone who has contributed in one way or the other to this book but I would like to start by thanking my PHD thesis Supervisor, **Dr Franklin Valcin**, who supported me in the completion of my PHD thesis - whose headline data and insights are discussed in the book.

Many HR practitioners that have gone ahead of me and contributed to the HR profession have also greatly influenced my interest in the profession as well as how I engage in HR practice. Special mention goes to **Dave Ulrich, Michael Armstrong and Wayne BrockBank**; who through their books and articles have challenged my understanding of HR practice and helped me to sharpen my knowledge of the Human Resource field. Also worthy of mention are the many Human Resource practice institutions that have helped shape and raise the bar in HR practice. These include **SHRM (USA), CIPD (UK), CHRODA (Botswana) and IHRM (Kenya)**.

Also worthy of mention are HR colleagues that have played willing peer coaches at various points in my career. *Andrew*

Thompson, Roy Masamba, Carol Auma, Eve Banda, Gloria Byamugisha, Milton Owor, Lyn Mengich, Alban Mwendar, Yves Mayilamene, and Dickson Ojukwu–your coaching has made me a better HR professional. To the CEOs, Line Managers and HR professionals across Africa who participated in the research work for this book, do accept my sincere gratitude.

Special thanks go to Combert Impressions for the cover design and print layout of the book.

INTRODUCTION

Much of the HR literature available today is focused on Europe, the United States and recently some of the emerging markets including India, China and Brazil. Not much literature is available on HR practice in Africa and definitely not on the behavioural skills development arena. Unlike in Europe, USA, Canada and other developed economies, information on the state of HR practice in Africa has largely remained unexplored.

Globally, the Human Resource function has been receiving a lot of attention and, probably more than any other business function, has undergone tremendous transformation. The function is no longer battling for recognition and it is time it delivered what it promised in its quest for a place at the table–value creation. It almost feels as if HR has come of age and for HR practitioners, it is an exciting time to be in the profession. The expectation is that HR will step up to its new role and lead organisations to sustain top-line business growth and bottom line profitability. HR practices have to seamlessly integrate with business strategy and at the same time facilitate organisational capability development leading to competitive advantage. In the midst of this opportunity, Vickers (2007) believes that the Human Resource function is not adjusting fast enough to tackle the challenges in the business environment. However, although there is a need to speed up HR transformation to take on the new role; to be effective, such speed has to be balanced with a need for collaboration with key stakeholders and it should be done through an inclusive approach.

In addition, the HR function ought to ensure that change in the organisation is driven at a rate at which the organisation can absorb and adjust to. If the capacity to absorb change is low, HR ought to work on increasing this capacity first before engaging in transformational change processes.

To deliver on its promise, the HR function has to take up a leadership role and acknowledge that what has been previously referred to as "strategic HR" is in itself changing and this transformation is taking place at a very fast pace. Ordinarily, when leadership is discussed, it is in reference to individuals or positions but in the case of Human Resources the entire function, and not just some of the positions, is being called upon to take on a leadership role. This places a fresh demand on HR professionals to stand up and embrace the clout that has been bestowed on the function.

Changes in the business arena including globalisation, adoption of technology, off shoring and outsourcing, increased competition, rising customer demands and glaring talent shortages have all accelerated the focus on the function that manages people; the Human Resource function. With the increased realisation that the Human Resource function can be a source of competitive advantage, an almost laser-like focus is being turned on to both the function and the occupants of positions in Human Resources.

One other thing - the HR function serves as the culture custodian and is normally viewed as the conscience of the organisation. As Pomeroy (2006) states, "The buck does stop at the HR's door". With this responsibility, additional demands are placed on the HR function to operate at a higher moral ground than other functions in the organisation. This can also be explained by the fact that the nature of the function exposes HR practitioners to a lot of confidential information. It has always been a tricky role for HR to act as an employee advocate while partnering the CEO in delivering the business plan.

HR Inspirational Tension

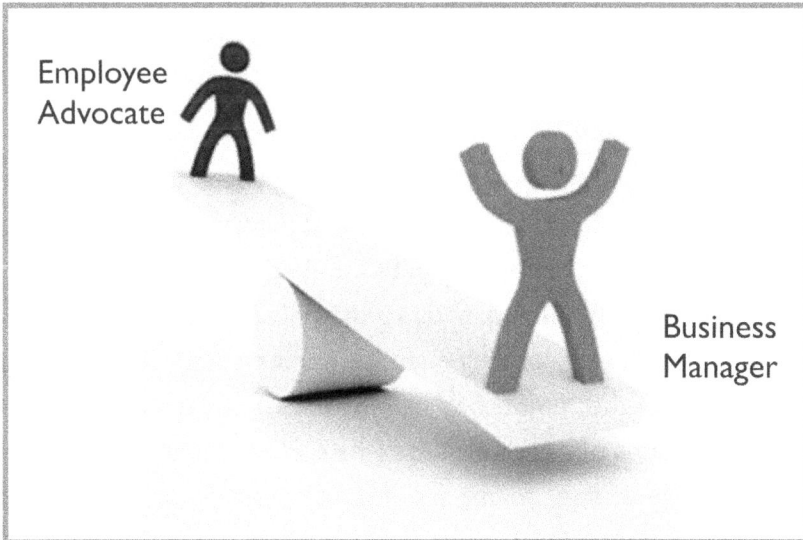

Employee Advocate

Business Manager

The sea saw is constantly viewed as being skewed to one side or the other leading to dissatisfaction and at times mistrust from either party. The HR professional has to master the art of maintaining this balance. This mastery calls for HR practitioners to be equipped with the skills to match the demands being placed on them.

Business leaders are calling for bigger, better and faster pace of organisational transformation in response to market demands. With the demand being placed on HR departments to deliver results at a much higher level and at an increased speed, the skill set of the HR professional has become an area of concern. The gap between the skills of the HR professional 20 years or even 10 years ago and those needed today and for the future is quite significant (Ulrich et al., 2008).

A review of literature indicates that the voice of fellow HR professionals is the one that seems to fills the "air waves" in regard to what skills are needed for HR to perform its new role and there is little in terms of voice from the other key stakeholders such as the CEO and Line managers or an opportunity to contribute to this ongoing debate. This gap will be addressed by taking a wholistic view and incorporating the views of these three stakeholders (CEO, HR and line managers) to provide the much needed input so that HR skill set development is not just an inward looking exercise (over criticism–navel gazing or self praise–the "emperor's new clothes") but is rather driven by the demands of key customers (the CEO for shareholders and investors; and line managers for employees and the end customer/communities).

Leadership is all about influence and if HR is to play a leadership role, HR professionals will need to be equipped with leadership skills. As Maxwell (2003) states, "true leadership cannot be awarded, appointed or assigned" as it comes from influence. The skill of influencing, like many other leadership skills, is a behavioural rather than a technical skill. Such behavioural skills are at times referred to as leadership competencies or soft skills. Developing soft skills will get HR professionals to the point where they are truly strategic and can put to rest the comments by Birchfield (2003) that, "there are a lot of HR practitioners out there but not many true HR leaders".

To give you an overview of the book, **Part I** explores the literature on human resource competencies and seeks to highlight why behavioural skills are absolutely crucial for the success of an HR professional. The HR function is the first and last point of contact for any employee in an organisation and the experience generated by that contact remains ingrained in an employee's mind years after leaving an organisation. This section discusses in detail the competency/skill expectations of HR professionals as proposed by leading human resource practitioners and researchers.

In **part 2**, the focus is on two of the key stakeholders of the HR professional; the CEO and the Line Manager. The three pillars for building a great organisation where talent thrives are the CEO, the HR professional and the line manager. These three stakeholders create the "employee experience" and effectively the culture of an organisation.

> *In very simplistic terms, the CEO can be said to be the head of an organisation - the visionary thinker providing direction; HR professionals – the heart and conscience taking care of the culture and employee wellbeing; and Line Managers – the mouth, translating strategy in to day to day execution requirements to deliver results.*

How HR interacts with these two stakeholders determines the level of influence the HR function will have on how employees experience the organisation on a day to day basis.

Part three is a review of HR behavioural skill development based on research data. The research reveals the current state of behavioural skill development within the HR fraternity in Africa and reviews the effectiveness of development approaches that are currently in use. A discussion centered on some of the development options available for up skilling HR professionals outlines some of the benefits and shortcomings that accrue from using different routes for skill development.

In **Part four**, a detailed skill development guide is provided to help HR practitioners to engage in self development and upskill their behavioural competencies. Prior to exploring the skill development options, a behavioural skills self assessment questionnaire is provided to help each individual identify their current strengths and skill gap areas.

Part five reviews the impact behavioural skills have on HR professionals and unpacks the assertion that the "buck does stop with HR"! If an organisation is not performing to expectations, a good look at HR–its leaders, the structure, the competencies in the function and the HR policies and practices will provide a good diagnosis of some of the strategies that need to change.

In **Part Six**, the ongoing evolution in Human Resource practice and the future of the function is discussed. There are clear pointers that in the future, the technical aspects of HR (the Hardware–Resourcing, Reward, Learning and Development, HRIS management, etc) will be less important as they could be outsourced to industry specialist firms and what organisations will retain as a core skill in HR would be HR Relationship Management (the software). HR Relationship Managers would have the sole responsibility of helping the organisation to nurture talent and create an unforgettable employee experience.

My hope is that this book will give you a new perspective, a better insight into the developments taking place within the profession and probably challenge you to relook at how you practice HR or how HR is practiced in your organisation.

It is time to step up to this new mandate and lead the change towards the new reality of Human Resource practice. You could be the HR leader we have been waiting for!

Part One

Why Behaviour is Crucial for the Success of The HR Professional

The term "behavioural competency" and "soft skill", though slightly different, are used interchangeably in this book. A competency is defined as the behaviour that employees must have in order to effectively perform their jobs (CIPD, 2010). Competencies or behavioural skills are very useful because they provide an organisation with a common language to discuss performance and give guidelines to employees about what an organisation values and rewards.

The International Encyclopedia of the social sciences (2008) defines soft skills as:

"Core abilities and personal attributes that complement hard skills; that is technical knowledge of an individual in the work place"

The effective use of soft skills is an indicator of the success of a leader and the HR profession needs to equip its professionals rather quickly with such leadership skills. In fact soft skills have become so Important, Wolosky (2008) states that such skills were once referred to as soft skills because they were thought to be less important than technical or hard skills but are now considered as the core skills. In a study by Ulrich et al., (2008), it was determined that management has about a 50% influence on an organisation's performance with the remaining 50% being outside management's control. Of the 50% impact under management control which includes strategy, marketing, etc, Human Resource accounts for 20% of the impact.

Given this level of potential impact by HR, the skills needed in the function go beyond technical or professional capabilities (such as

Compensation & Benefits management, Change management, Training and Development, Employee Relations, Resourcing) and stretch to other skills that drive overall organisational performance. HR is being called upon to play the role of an internal performance consultant for the organisation, and it is such skills required by HR professionals that will be explored in this book.

To effectively support the business to deliver value, HR capabilities can be measured on three fronts; whether the function has the necessary technical competencies such as change management, talent management, reward management, operational skills; whether the people working within HR have the required soft skills (also referred to as behavioural skills); and the structure of the function. If these three aspects are in place and well managed, then HR is strategically placed to drive and lead business performance.

Drivers of a successful HR Function

4

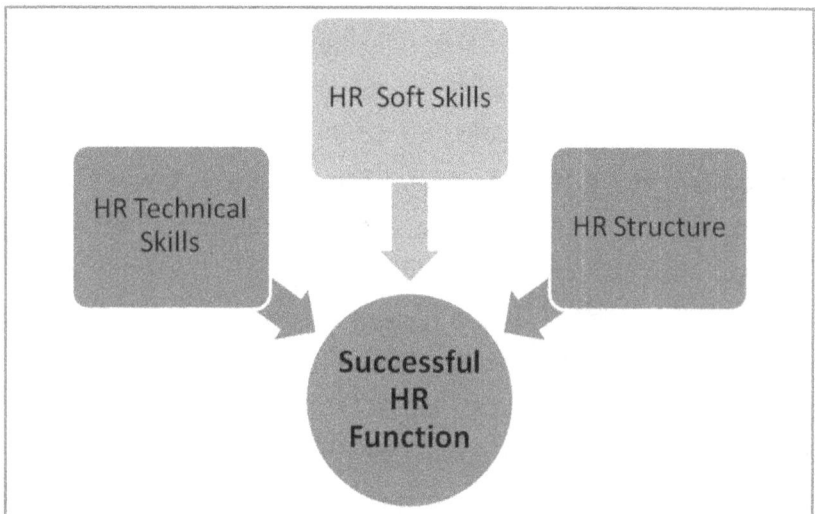

HR Soft Skills

HR Technical Skills

HR Structure

Successful HR Function

To use a simple analogy to explain these three drivers: the technical skills (Talent Management, Resourcing, Learning and Development, Change Management) could be compared to various parts of a car for example the engine, steering wheel, the tyres, the gear box and so on; the structure of the HR function would be likened to the assembly of the car parts in their appropriate places so they can function well; and the soft skills would be the nuts, bolts and glue that holds all the parts together in their right place.

Without the right parts (technical competencies) you don't have a car in much the same way as an individual attempting to practice HR without the preliquisite knowledge (and we unfortunately do see a lot of this in organisations today!). If the parts are wrongly placed while assembling the car (the HR structure), the final product may look like a car but it will not function properly. Back office functions expected to perform front office work is a good example of this misalignment. If the bolts are weak or are missing the car will fall apart (soft skills). If the parts are not well oiled as the car moves the squeaking experienced is a distraction and causes unnecessary "noise" in the system. Soft skills are the equivalent of nuts, bolts and glue that ensure harmony, collaboration and team work in the organisation eliminating the "noise" that tends to distract focus from performance. An organisation's potential to deliver results is affected by the level of distraction and interruptions and this leads to less than optimal results even when an organisation has highly talented individuals. The HR function has to master the art of identifying noise, interruptions and distractions in the organisation and minimizing or eliminating them to provide a supportive environment that fosters high performance.

The need to transform the HR function has been a result of the realisation that employees actually represent "human capital" (Armstrong, 2006) and can present a unique source of competitive advantage to an organisation. Analysis carried out by Lengnick-Hall et al., (2009) indicates that the transformation that has been taking place in the Human Resource Management (HRM) field could be equated to an evolution with the drive for change coming from three sources; an internal drive, external contexts as well as the interplay between the two. There has been a clear shift from the previous debate around whether Human Resource Management makes a difference in the organisation to how this difference can be managed, leveraged and augmented.

With all the discussions taking place about HRM, its role and the impact it is having or should have in organisations, it is as though the HR function is suffering from a "confidence crisis" (Torrington, 1998). This seeming crisis in the function has actually provided an opportunity for HR practitioners to step up in their role and prove their ability to add value to the business. Business impact is what the HR function needs to focus on in order to mature to the level of other decision sciences such as Finance and Marketing (Lawler, et al., 2006). You will barely ever hear Finance Directors having a conversation around whether they add any value to the business, they know they do and the organisations accept that without question. What will it take for HR practice to "mature" to this level?

Ehlrich (1997) intimates that HR adds value in the business by creating an employee-friendly organisation. This is effectively carried out through HR professionals building relationships in the business and being an advocate of employee issues. However, to carry out this role, certain skills are required and it is the lack of such skills that contributes to HR ineffectiveness (Aitchison, 2007). HR soft skills are the missing ingredient needed to propel the profession to a position of influence and impact.

Because of the significant shift in the roles that the HR function is expected to play in the organisation, developing new skills remains a crucial step in achieving the promise that HR has transformed in to a value-adding function (Lawler and Mohrman, 2003). A lot of debate and research has already gone in to the identification of the competencies needed by the competent HR professional. Much of this work has resulted in advocating for competencies that cover both the business aspects and the individual behaviours of HR professionals.

According to CIPD (2009), HR competencies can be divided in to three inter-related sets:

▶ The knowledge needed or technical competencies e.g. Change Management or Employee Relations
▶ The activities that HR needs to engage in e.g. conducting talent reviews or implementing recognition schemes
▶ The behaviours needed in order to be effective

HR Competency Studies

Dave Ulrich, in conjunction with the Society of Human Resource Management (SHRM), has been carrying out HR competency studies under the HR Competency Studies (HRCS) series since 1987 and the findings indicate that these competencies have evolved in line with the expectations placed on the function. The findings of the various studies have been shared with the HR profession in conferences, articles, journals and books. In Ulrich et al., (2008) the entire evolution of the competencies is presented through the various HRCS studies under what are referred to as rounds of study. The first study was carried out in 1987 and three competencies were identified as critical for HR success namely **business knowledge, change** and **HR delivery**. The results of the round 2 study of 1992 indicated that these three competencies were still considered critical but a fourth competence had emerged—**personal credibility**. Round 3 HRCS study of 1997 maintained the four competencies: **HR delivery, change, business knowledge, personal credibility** and a fifth competence; **culture**, was identified as crucial for the HR profession.

Round 4 HRCS Model

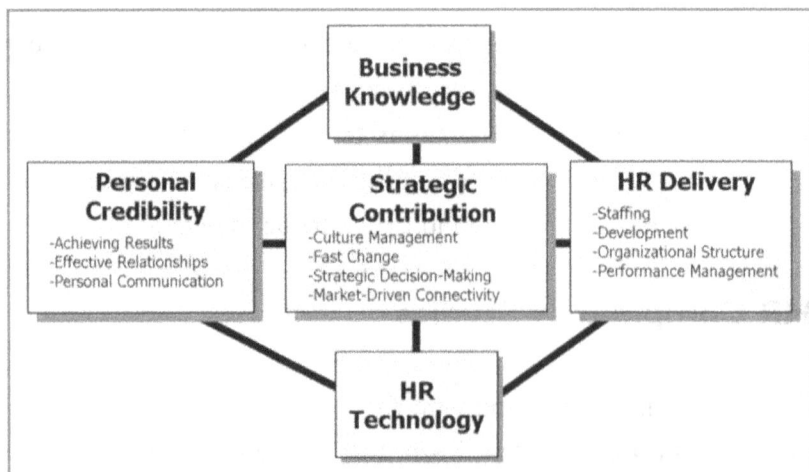

Source: Boselie, P & Paauwe, J. (2004)

In the Round 4 study carried out in 2002 (refer to Figure), a new competency emerged, **HR technology**. The HR technology competence supports the HR professional to effectively carry out transactional work and also provide analytics to drive the operational excellence of the function. During the same round, the **culture** and **change** competencies were combined under a new competency referred to as **Strategic contribution**. In this round of study, **strategic contribution** and **personal credibility** were identified as contributing over 60% to individual and business performance.

Under the 5th round of the HRCS (refer to figure), being a **credible activist** was identified as the most crucial competence to both the individual and the organisation. Being a credible activitist goes beyond personal credibility and means that the HR professional has a point of view on business issues and effectively speaks out to articulate this view. The next set of competencies in importance after credible activist, were identified as **talent management, culture & change steward and strategy architect**.

9

Round 5 HR Competency model

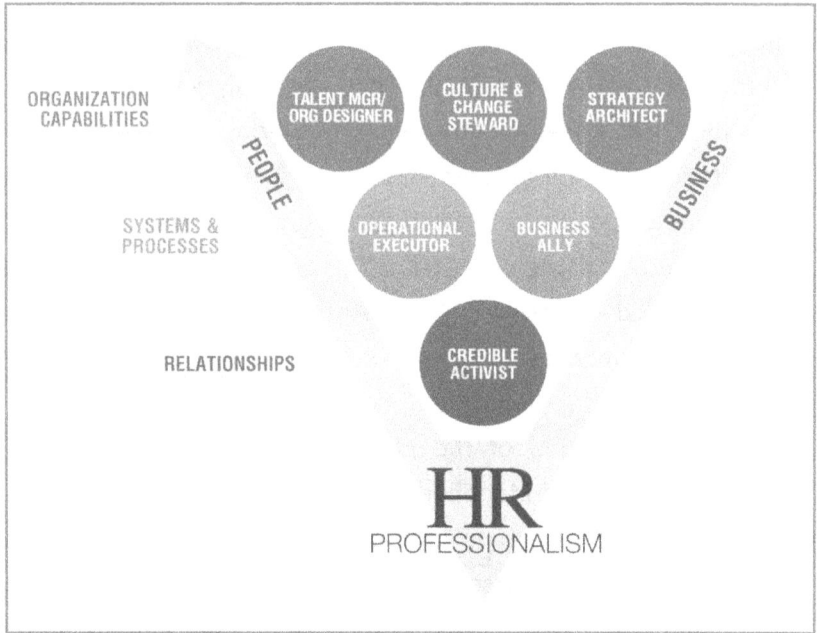

Source: Ulrich et al., (2008), pg 37

10 **Operational executor and business ally** were identified as competences that may not have a high impact on organisational capability but their delivery gives the HR professional the "right" to discuss the strategic issues of the business. With this latest study and the confirmation that the credible activist competence was the most crucial, it brings to the fore the increasing importance of behavioural competencies in the HR profession. It is this increasing importance placed on soft skills that makes it imperative to equip the HR professional of today with such skills as they are key drivers for success.

HR Behavioural Skills (soft skills)

Some work has already been done in identifying the behavioural skills required by the HR professional. The Chartered Institute of Personnel Development (CIPD) has been exploring a radical change in the process of equipping the profession to meet the challenges that lie ahead (People Management, 2009). The thrust of the work by the CIPD is meant to ensure the profession remains relevant and equipped to play its role with excellence. The institute has identified eight behaviours under three main sub themes or output expectations: **insights and influence, stewardship and operational excellence**. Under each of these sub themes, specific behavioural competencies have been identified as contributors under each sub-theme.

CIPD HR Behavioural Skills

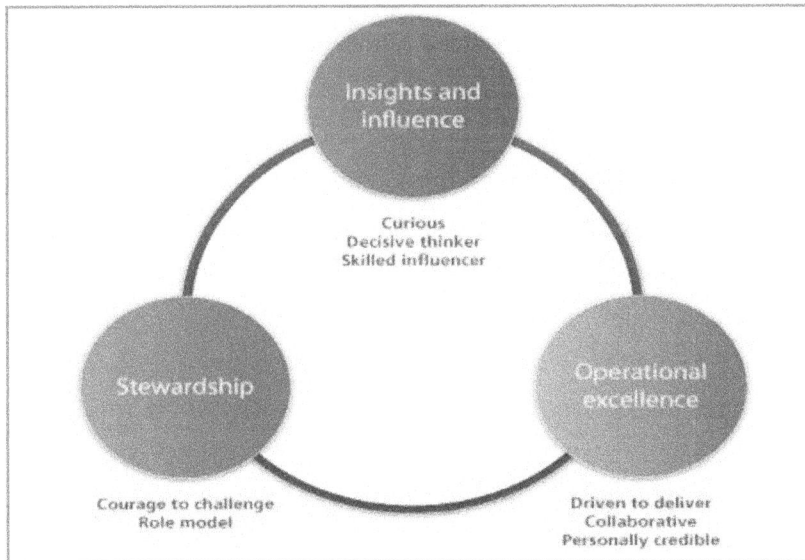

Insights and influence

Curious
Decisive thinker
Skilled influencer

Stewardship

Operational excellence

Courage to challenge
Role model

Driven to deliver
Collaborative
Personally credible

Source: CIPD website; www.cipd.co.uk

11

The CIPD lists eight behaviours as critical for an HR practitioner: **Curious, Decisive Thinker, Skilled influencer** (Insights and influence), **Driven to deliver, Collaborative, Personally Credible** (operational excellence), Courage to challenge and Role Model (stewardship).

Other organisations too have come up with sets of behaviours expected of their HR teams. Oxfam GB (2005) lists the following as critical HR behaviours: **Attention to details, Effective communication, Analytical, Flexible, Self management, influencing others, Customer service, Drive for results and Relationship management.** Skills such as Courage, Curiosity and being Caring are gaining credence as core skills for someone working in the HR profession (Meisenger, 2005). Other behaviours have been identified as key for HR practitioners such as Accessibility and embracing Inclusiveness.

Due to the interconnectedness of the different functions within the organisation in the delivery of customer service, the need to build strong relationships cannot be over emphasised. The way an individual behaves has a great impact on their general effectiveness as it influences the reactions and actions of team members and colleagues. For HR professionals, the importance of behaviour is even more amplified. This is because HR as the custodian of culture in an organisation has far reaching impact on employee engagement and overall productivity. HR directly influences the culture of an organisation and effectively the ability to attract and retain talent, the level of employee loyalty and the general trust levels in the organisation.

An initial analysis of the key HR behaviours advocated for by different organisations indicated some level of overlap and a final list (though not fully exhaustive) was drawn up for further research. The behavioural skills list used for this research is presented below.

HR Behavioural Skills

Behavioural Skills List		
Accessible	Confident	Decisive
Analytical	Courageous to Challenge	Visionary
Attention to Details	Collaborative	Curious
Caring	Effective Communicator	Driven to Deliver
Skilled Influencer	Customer Oriented	Flexible
Personally Credible	Relationship Builder	

13

Behaviour descriptors

A brief definition and discussion of each behaviour and its contribution is provided below. Depending on the organisation and the role an individual HR professional is playing, each skill takes on a different level of importance and priority.

▶ **Accessible** - the ability to be approachable, preferring face to face communication and displaying true humility. The push to implement open door policies is driven by a need to be more accessible. An HR professional who is not accessible will lose touch with the employees in the organisation and will not be effective in inculcating the desired culture. An HR professional who is accessible will receive input and feedback from employees and line managers and will be in a better position to tailor HR initiatives to the needs of stakeholders.

▶ **Analytical -** the ability to consider multiple aspects of a proposal, problem or initiative in an objective, logical and systematic way. Analytical diagnosis provides authentic input for informing decision making. Without this skill set, the HR practitioner will incorporate limited perspectives and the resulting proposals may not stand the test of a rigorous review process. In addition, without proper analysis, initiatives introduced will tend to be short term in approach and "flavour of the month" and may not stand the test of time.

▶ **Attention to details -** the ability to complete work using a systematic approach of testing the quality of work such that the incidence of error is much reduced or is within acceptable standards. HR as a function has received much criticism about its inability to provide basic data including headcount numbers. Such incidences lead to HR data being viewed with skeptism reducing the ability of the HR function to influence business decisions.

▶ **Caring -** the ability to value people and the contribution they make to an organisation. This means that HR is expected to consider the impact a decision will have on employees. This does not mean that HR will oppose any decision that would have a negative impact on people e.g. job loss, but rather that HR needs to get creative and propose ways of minimizing the negative impact of such decisions.

▶ *Skilled Influencer* - the ability to convince others to follow a particular course of action. This includes the ability to generate debate around issues that matter to an individual. The level of influence is critical to an HR practitioner as it directly impacts the delivery of the HR agenda. At times, it is not that HR professionals do not have solutions for problems in organisations, but rather that their voice is not heard leading to lost opportunities.

▶ *Personally Credible* - this is the degree of "believability" or the degree of being thought of as trustworthy. Trust is possibly one of the most critical attributes that can be bestowed on an HR practitioner as it is directly linked to their perceived character. The need for personal credibility explains why today the top competence for a person in a leadership position is integrity.

15

▶ *Confident* - describes certainty that a course of action, a decision or an approach is the correct one under particular circumstances. Confidence is a crucial skill for leaders and improves the ability to get buy-in for proposals. This does not mean that a confident person is presumptuous or arrogant. Such confidence could come from previous experience or a deep belief emanating from accurate diagnosis.

▶ **Courageous to challenge** - this is the ability to do the right thing when one is under pressure to do a different thing. Such courage to challenge comes from confidence in ones competence. Courage to challenge is closely linked with ethics and HR professionals who don't speak up when unethical practices are taking place eventually dilute the strength of the organisational culture.

▶ **Collaborative** - the ability to champion an environment of teamwork and a spirit of cooperation while removing barriers to team effectiveness. For HR professionals to succeed, they need to elicit support from a broad range of stakeholders who many times have competing demands. A collaborative approach assures cooperation is given in a climate of respect.

▶ **Effective communicator** - the ability to give clear messages or information using a variety of medium (oral or written) whilst appreciating the needs of the audience. It is said that communication, much like the culture in an organisation, is one of the key pillars for organisational effectiveness. HR professionals need to master the art of communication in order to be effective.

▶ **Customer orientated** - the ability to pick out customer insights, anticipate the needs of the customer and design processes that are geared at satisfying the customer. Although the main customer of HR is the internal customer, the demands such internal customers place on HR are effectively driven by the need of the external customer. HR professionals who are customer orientated come up with processes that simplify the lives of internal customers therefore releasing valuable time to deal with external customer demands.

▶ *Relationship builder* - the ability to identify, develop, nurture and maintain productive interactions with key stakeholders. It takes time and effort to build productive relationships but the alternative which is a conflict prone environment is not a viable choice. For a relationship to develop there has to be sincere acknowledgement of each party in the relationship. HR professionals should be proactive in building such relationships as they effectively pave the way for speed in implementing business initiatives.

▶ *Decisive* - the ability to exercise good judgment and make sound decisions. This is not about making rush decisions that have no backing. Indecisive HR professionals will demand large amounts of data or evidence before making a decision. In the meantime, a work situation could deteriorate beyond a point where it can be successfully restored. The ability to use logic and extrapolate possible outcomes will help the HR practitioner to become more decisive.

▶ *Curious* - the ability to remain inquisitive about trends in the industry, in the business and in the external environment. This curiosity helps maintain a stock of knowledge of current challenges, new trends and opportunities that could be a source of competitive advantage for the organisation. In addition, curiosity ensures HR professionals effectively play their role of business partner and remain up to date on stakeholder priorities leading to the design of interventions that are relevant to stakeholders. Curiosity also helps keep the HR professional relevant to the organisation.

▶ **_Driven to deliver_** - the ability to develop, deliver and achieve creative solutions in a timely manner to support and enhance the business. It is about setting clear milestones and targets for work and meeting them. An HR professional who is driven to deliver will make promises and follow them through to completion. To deliver results on time, one has to be proactive, anticipate blockages and come up with alternative approaches for achieving results.

▶ **_Flexible_** - the ability to act within the existing decision making framework while remaining open to new evidence. Such flexibility is not the same as being indecisive but rather it is the ability to expand options and possible solutions thereby improving critical reasoning capability. Many times HR professionals are said to be inflexible and only willing to follow the HR policy "by the book". Incorporating some flexibility and acknowledging that policy can and should change to pave the way for better outcomes will keep HR professionals open to creative solutions that may lie outside current policies and approaches.

▶ **_Visionary_** - the ability to paint a positive picture of the future and influence people to desire that future. It requires a good understanding of the internal and the external context as well as an ability to employ an integrative perspective. This leads to the ability to spot cross cutting themes and effectively build sources of distinction that are not easy to imitate. This skill is critical for HR professionals when designing the HR strategy and being visionary does lead to the development of competitive advantage.

Having gone through the definitions of each of the behavioural skills and prior to getting the CEO and Line Manager stakeholder perspective on HR behavioural skill levels, a self assessment of your individual current skill level would help focus your learning and ensure you get the most out of this book.

There are three broad approaches to skill development:

- **Identifying areas of weakness and working to improve them.** Right from our early school days we got used to receiving report cards with scores on various subjects. Most of us would focus on the lowest scored subjects and worry about our low competence levels. Our parents were highly likely to enroll us in a tuition class to help improve low scores. Some of us still follow this approach to self development today.

- **Identifying your strengths and working towards raising further the skill levels.** This school of personal development believes that we are better off working on what we are already good at and becoming great at it rather than spending time working on weaknesses. There is value in this approach as everyone does possess an area of strength that can be further strengthened to produce next to flawless performance.

- **Working around the competence you desire to develop.** This is akin to the cross-training that sportsmen use. For example, a marathon runner will of course take time to practice their running but they will also do some weight lifting, maybe some aerobics or swimming; all meant to strengthen them without injuring their muscles through running longer and longer distances every day.

All the above approaches are valid and probably a combination of the three would lead to the best results. Identifying areas of weakness and working to improve them to a point where they no longer stand in the way of your performance; identifying areas of strength and turning them to absolute excellence; and working on other skills that indirectly support your strengths. The skill development guide provided in Part four will provide you with tips and strategies for developing your skills along these three approaches.

The self assessment questionnaire below will help you identify your areas of improvement and your areas of strengths.

Behavioural skills self-assessment questionnaire

In responding to this questionnaire place yourself in the shoes of your CEO, the line managers you work with or colleagues in HR department and determine how they would score you. If you are not yet working in an HR role, give yourself a self score based on feedback you have received from colleagues or you could use your own objective assessment.

With 1 (one) being poor and 10 (ten) being excellent, indicate how you think the above stakeholders would score you on these behavioural skills (refer to the definitions of behavioural competencies provided previously).

Behavioural Skills Self Assessment (BSSA)

Behavioural Skill	Self Score									
	1	2	3	4	5	6	7	8	9	10
Accessible										
Analytical										
Confident										
Caring										
Flexible										
Courageous to challenge										
Customer oriented										
Driven to deliver										
Effective communicator										
Skilled influencer										
Collaborative										
Curious										
Visionary										
Relationship builder										
Decisive										
Personally credible										
Attentive to details										

Complete the learning journal below based on your scores on the behavioural skill questionnaire above.

1. Did you score a 4 or below in any of the behavioural skills? (these are the areas of improvement). If so, list those behavioural skills here.

   ....
   ....
   ....
   ....
   ....
   ....

2. Did you score an 8 or above on any of the behavioural skills? (these are your strengths). If so, list those behavioural skills here.

   ....
   ....
   ....
   ....
   ....
   ....

There are other skills where you scored between a 5 and a 7. These skills are neutral in terms of contributing to your success. If you don't have any identified strength (score 8-10) or would like to single out some of the skills in this category for further development, please list them below.

....

....

....

....

....

....

As you go through the rest of the sections, keep referring to your Behavioural Skill Self Assessment (BSSA) as it will help you focus your development on areas that will bring you immediate on-the-job impact.

23

Part Two

MANAGING STAKEHOLDERS

Human Resource practice is fascinating when carried out professionally but can go horribly wrong if left in the hands of a novice. Unlike assets such as machines, or finances, people–the key resource for HR practitioners, have the ability to talk back, to argue, reason and actually walk away or walk out of an organisation. This makes managing people interesting and calls for a certain "type" of a person to carry out the HR role.

Based on the seventeen behavioural competencies introduced earlier, a survey was conducted targeting CEOs, Line Managers and HR professionals. The focus of the survey was to gather information on which of the competencies contribute to the success of an HR professional and also to get a perspective on how HR professionals are rated on these competencies. The survey was restricted to African countries and mainly focused on four countries: Kenya, Nigeria, Ghana and South Africa.

Profile of respondents	
Respondent Type	**Response Percentage**
CEO/GENERAL MANAGER	10%
LINE MANAGER	28%
HR PROFESSIONAL	62%
TOTAL	**100%**

Source: Research data, 2010

A larger proportion of respondents (62%) were HR professionals and this provides a good insight in to the subject of study from actual practitioners that understand the intricacies of the profession. Line managers made up 28% of respondents and CEO's a further 10%.

The overall top skills identified by respondents as being at the centre of perceived effectiveness of HR professionals are: **Effective communication, Relationship builder and Personally credible.**

Priority Skill Scores for HR Success

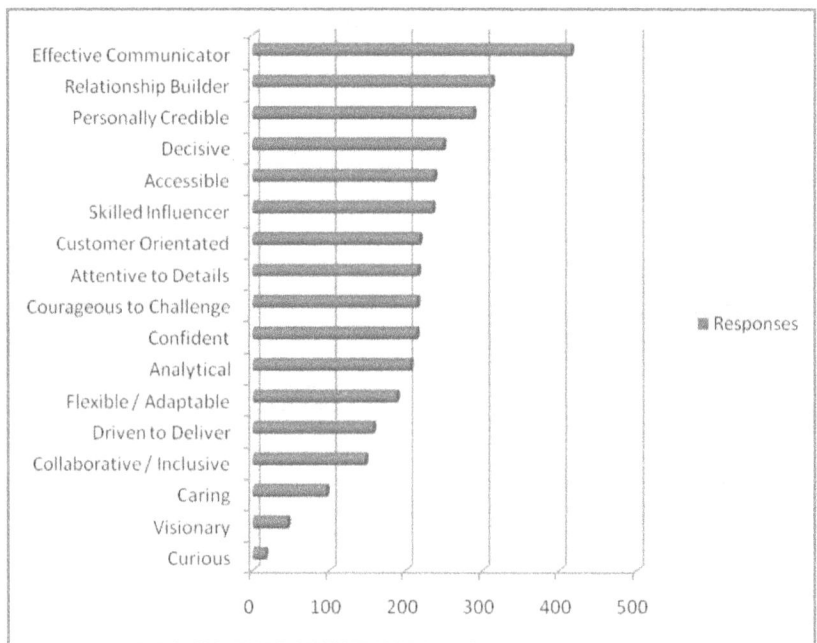

Source: Research data, 2010

Apart from the top 3 skills identified *(Effective Communication, Personally Credible, Relationship builder)*, other behavioural skills voted as high contributors of success included **Decisive, Accessible, Skilled Influencer, Customer Orientated, Attentive to Details, Courageous to Challenge** and **Confident**. An important point to note is that the respondents overwhelmingly identified effective communicator as the number one skill for HR professional success. If only one behavioural skill could be incorporated into a selection process for an HR professional, then that would be **Effective Communication**.

Overall Current Skill Levels

The Likert Scale was used to analyze the current behavioural skill level; as scored by the various stakeholders, (with 1 denoting below average, 2 for average, 3 representing above average and 4 for excellent). This analysis reveals the score card given to HR professionals along the various skills. HR professionals are said to be best at being **accessible** with an average score of 2.89, followed by **personally credible** (2.74) and confident (2.73) levels. The next three skills with high scores for HR practitioners include **effective communicator** (2.6), **driven to deliver** (2.55) and **attention to details** (2.53).

Current Skill level of HR Professionals

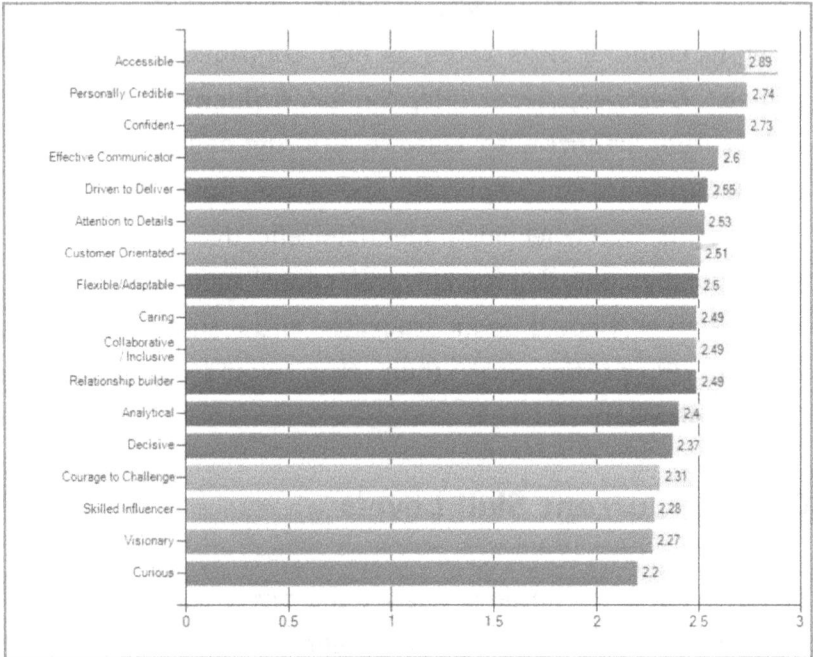

Accessible	2.89
Personally Credible	2.74
Confident	2.73
Effective Communicator	2.6
Driven to Deliver	2.55
Attention to Details	2.53
Customer Orientated	2.51
Flexible/Adaptable	2.5
Caring	2.49
Collaborative / Inclusive	2.49
Relationship builder	2.49
Analytical	2.4
Decisive	2.37
Courage to Challenge	2.31
Skilled Influencer	2.28
Visionary	2.27
Curious	2.2

Source: Research Data, 2010

30

The research findings confirm that accessibility of the HR professional is ranked highest as a skill that HR professionals have mastered. This is good news for the HR professional since in the past under Personnel management; a call to report to the personnel office triggered fear and uncertainty for employees (could it be a warning letter, termination, caution!). That said, there is still a lot of improvement expected in this area and the ongoing attempts to create "front office HR" or HR Business partners will help in addressing this gap. HR plays the critical role of translating business strategy in to the HR agenda and simultaneously cascading this to the rest of the business. As culture custodians, HR professionals are expected to constantly interact with stakeholders not only to ensure that the organisational culture is aligned to business objectives but also to onboard new employees in to the organisation and counsel those that are not living the organisational values.

The personal credibility of HR professionals is also ranked quite high (2.74) which is great news as credibility is what gives the function the ticket to contribute to strategy formulation. A low score on personal credibility would cast a real shadow on the ability of HR professionals to influence the business agenda. Employees want to be led by a person and not by a position and this is where the importance of personal credibility of HR professionals comes to play. Where personal credibility is lacking, positional authority will tend to be invoked to gain compliance and this does not augur well for building a culture where employees give of their best.

A comparison between the skills identified as a priority for HR success and those that HR practitioners are currently rated highly reveals some gaps. These gaps can be a source of frustration within the business as what stakeholders of the HR function expect may not be delivered as a result of low levels of competency.

Priority Skills	Skills with High Scores
Effective Communication	Accessible
Relationship Builder	Personally Credible
Personally Credible	Confident

Source: Research Data, 2010

The survey results indicate that HR professionals are getting high scores in behavioural skills that are essential for their success but that are not ranked as critical success factors. The only exception to this is **personally credible** that appears on both lists. This insight presents an opportunity for HR professionals to prioritize skill development in the priority areas of **effective communication and relationship building**.

A comparison of the survey results across the stakeholders indicates some congruence between the CEO, Line Managers and HR professionals, but also some points of departure in terms of prioritisation.

Stakeholder Behavioural Skill Priorities

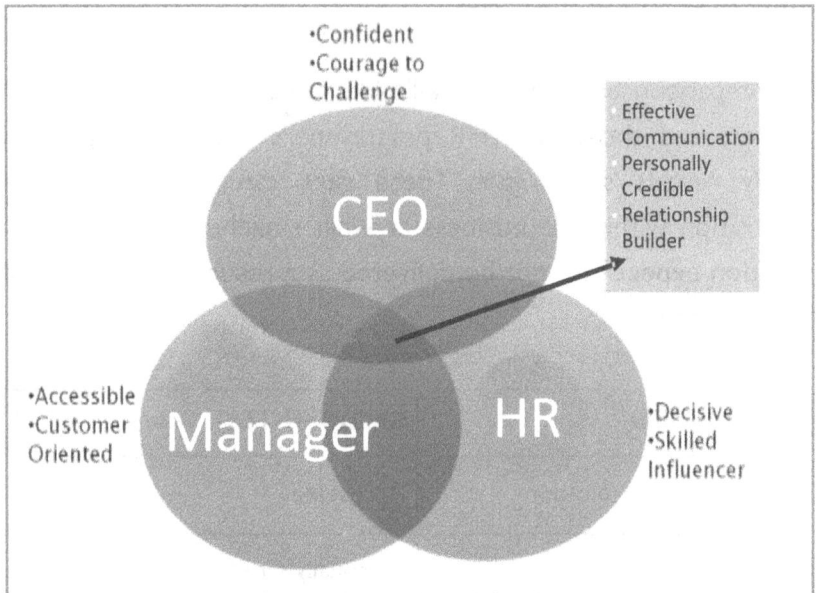

·Confident
·Courage to
Challenge

Effective
Communication
Personally
Credible
Relationship
Builder

CEO

·Accessible
·Customer
Oriented

Manager

HR

·Decisive
·Skilled
Influencer

Source: Research Data, 2010

The three stakeholders agree that *Effective Communication, Relationship Building* and *Personal Credibility* are important for the success of an HR professional. However, there are some additional skills each of the stakeholder's places in their top 5 skills. CEOs would like HR professionals to be **confident** and have the **courage to challenge**. Line managers' single out being **accessible** and **customer orientation** as additional priority skills and HR professionals flag up being **decisive** and being a **skilled influencer** as additional priorities.

Before discussing the detailed scorecards from each of the stakeholders, it would help to examine the relationships between the stakeholders. The relationship between the CEO and the HR Executive deserves special focus here. This relationship is akin to a dance of tango–a very close collaboration that requires real precision in alignment. When the relationship is working well, it is clear to all line managers and employees as there is congruence in employee messaging. On the contrary, when this relationship does not work well, just like a messy performance of tango; stepping on each other's toes and the pursuit of conflicting agendas ultimately leads to low trust levels in the organisation. If attempts to work on the relationship do not yield results, the best option is to amicably part ways for the good of the business.

The CEO Perspective

Behavioural Skill	Priority Level	Mean Scores
Effective Communicator	I	2.74
Personally Credible	2	2.65
Relationship Builder	3	2.63
Confident	4	2.81
Courage to Challenge	5	2.42

Source: Research Data, 2010

The behavioural skills prioritised by the CEO are *Effective Communicator, Personally Credible and Relationship Builder*. Given the central and strategic role of HR in translating organisation direction in to employee policies, a combination of these three skills places HR in a very good place to influence culture and the general organisational climate. The two additional skills identified by CEOs as important are quite linked; *Confident* and *Courage to Challenge*. In order for HR professionals to have the courage to challenge company direction or strategy, the job holders have to be quite confident in their own ability and competency as well as possess good knowledge of the business. It is what some HR authors refer to as doing HR "with an attitude". The fact that these two skills come up as a priority is not surprising given the earlier discussion on the nature of the CEO/HR relationship.

CEOs rely on the HR executive to provide the people perspective in the business and they value this perspective in decision making. From the results of the survey, although CEOs view HR professionals as relatively confident (2.81), the score for Courage to Challenge (2.42) is much lower and gives an indication of a skill gap that HR professionals should be targeting to upskill.

The HR Perspective

HR professionals' top 3 priorities mirror those of CEOs as demonstrated below. The two additional skills that are identified as priority by HR practitioners are *decisive* and *skilled influencer*.

HR Score Card

Behavioural Skill	Priority Level	Mean Scores
Effective Communication	I	2.68
Relationship Builder	2	2.57
Personally Credible	3	2.89
Decisive	4	2.39
Skilled Influencer	5	2.34

Source: Research Data, 2010

People decisions, unlike money decisions or other decisions that impact assets, can be quite emotive. The HR policy may be very clear but at times decisions have a negative impact on people and the HR professional has the difficult role of being both the "policy enforcer" and the "carer". This is a difficult balance to maintain and often times HR practitioners are said to be indecisive when the business needs to take tough decisions that impact employees. This in turn impacts on their personal credibility and relationship with key stakeholders.

Influencing is a skill HR practitioners identify as crucial for their effectiveness. They need to influence various stakeholders especially in times of transformation or while managing change. For HR professionals, learning the skill of influencing would have a significant impact on work effectiveness and the speed of project implementation. This, in turn, would have a positive impact on business performance.

These two additional skills (influencing and decisive) as singled out by HR practitioners as crucial would also have a significant positive impact on the top three skills (effective communication, personal credibility and relationship building). Possessing these additional skills would strengthen the core competencies leading to a higher level of contribution by HR practitioners in the business.

The Line Manager Perspective

The Line Manager is the real face of organisational culture due to the fact that their work impacts an employees' day to day experience. It is often said that this interaction is the moment of truth when it comes to an employee's connection with an organisation (where the rubber meets the road). It is therefore critical that a close collaboration is maintained between HR and Line Managers. Line managers are the mouth pieces of the company strategy and are the ones that manage day to day execution and if their message contradicts the organisational goals, the lack of alignment is likely to impact top line business results.

From the research data, the skill priority list for Line Managers deviates a little from that of the CEO and the HR professional. Although personal credibility still ranks in the top 5, it is given the lowest ranking priority whilst **accessibility** and **customer orientation** take precedence.

Line Manager Score Card

Behavioural Skill	Priority Level	Mean Scores
Effective Communication	1	2.4
Relationship Builder	2	2.28
Accessible	3	2.68
Customer Orientated	4	2.28
Personally Credible	5	2.47

Source: Research Data, 2010

For the Line Manager, accessibility of HR practitioners is crucial in order to ensure people issues are handled in a responsive manner. This is why the role of HR Business Partners (HRBP) is so important if the needs of this key stakeholder are to be met. HR functions that are yet to implement the HRBP model are denying line managers the support they need to improve people management. Creating HRBP roles is only the first step in this process; re-designing the role and ensuring accessibility, for example, by ensuring that HRBPs actually physically sit in the same space as the line managers they support is important. This is a real step in ensuring HR practitioners are perceived as accessible by Line Managers. HRBPs are the most effective when they are totally integrated in the departments they support is important. The ultimate measure of an excellent HRBP is when Line Managers relate with the HRBP as a core member of their function and blame "HR" when HR policy and practice goes wrong.

Line Managers are often charged with the responsibility of delighting the external customer and are used to adapting their processes and systems to suit customer needs. As internal customers of HR, at times Line Managers are disappointed that HR tends to be inflexible and sticks to a "rule book" and chooses to quote policies as the reason why certain actions cannot be taken even when it is clear that the policy in question is no longer applicable in the given situation. What Line Managers would like to see is an attempt by HR to continually review HR policy and ensure it is aligned to organisational plans and priorities rather than taking a reactive stand and only commence policy review when forced to by the circumstances.

To become customer oriented, HR would need to proactively review organisational policies and ensure they are supportive of what the organisation wants to achieve. The flexibility demonstrated by listening to internal customer feedback and responding with process and policy changes would demonstrate that HR has become a more customer oriented function.

Mean Scores on 9 top Skills across Stakeholders

Behavioural Skill	Mean Scores		
	CEOs	HR Professionals	Line Managers
Effective Communication	2.74	2.68	2.4
Personally Credible	2.65	2.89	2.47
Relationship builder	2.63	2.57	2.28
Confident	2.81	2.75	2.68
Courageous to challenge	2.42	2.37	2.15
Accessible	2.93	2.99	2.68
Customer Orientation	2.47	2.62	2.28
Decisive	2.51	2.39	2.27
Skilled Influencer	2.42	2.34	2.11

Source: Research Data, 2010

39

Of the top three skills identified by each of the respondents, HR professionals' performance is scored the lowest on the relationship builder skill. For the last 10-15 years or so there has been a general clamour for HR to become part of the strategy formulating team. This has largely been achieved and most Heads of HR sit in management committees for their organisation. The general congruence in the scores provided by both CEOs and HR professionals is a reflection of the closer alignment between the two stakeholders.

Of specific interest is that Line Managers ratings of HR professionals across all skills are the lowest of the three stakeholders. The results of this study indicate a gap between the expectations of HR professionals and those of the Line Manager. For HR to become more strategic, a lot of the administrative day to day activities have either been outsourced or placed in the Line Manager docket. The low ratings from the Line Manager could be emanating from a lack of understanding as to why HR has left what seems to be their "core" job to the Line Manager. To address this, HR professionals would need to ensure that there is a mutual stakeholder understanding around the roles and expectations between the two. As mentioned earlier, proper implementation of the HRBP would help in closing this gap.

Given that more and more of the day to day employee management activities will be delegated to the Line Manager including compensation and benefits decisions, hiring and firing decisions, motivation and performance management, the study highlights an opportunity for HR professionals to focus on building a close relationship with this crucial stakeholder. This would enhance the clarity needed between the two stakeholders and also build the skill of the Line Manager to carry out the people roles that have been "transferred" to them.

A Country View

From research data, it is evident that country culture has an impact on stakeholder expectations of HR professionals and in turn on the skill set that is critical for success. The survey results indicated that there were some differences in the prioritisation of behavioural skills of HR professionals in the context of the different countries. Kenya, Ghana, Nigeria and South Africa form the group of African countries that presented enough respondents to allow for this comparative analysis. The data from the research provides some interesting nuances that come in to play in the HR practice arena for each country.

Human behaviour is greatly influenced by the community and culture and there is no doubt that the expectations from each country in terms of behavioural skills priority can be explained by the respective country cultures.

Average Country Behavioural Skill Scores

Behavioural Skills	Average Scores and (Ranking *)			
	Kenya	Nigeria	South Africa	Ghana
Effective Communicator	2.66 (1)	2.45 (1)	2.21 (1)	2.59 (2)
Relationship Builder	2.52 (2)	2.13 (3)	2.28 (5)	2.62 (1)
Decisive	2.43 (3)	2.16 (Other)	1.79 (Other)	2.41(Other)
Personally Credible	2.84 (4)	2.34 (6)	2.28 (2)	3.12 (4)
Skilled Influencer	2.34 (5)	2.05 (Other)	2 (10)	2.22 (10)
Driven to Deliver	2.62 (Other)	2.29 (Other)	2.14 (9)	2.47 (5)
Courageous to challenge	2.32 (10)	2.13 (Other)	1.93 (4)	2.41 (Other)
Confident	2.77 (9)	2.58 (5)	2.45 (Other)	2.94(9)
Accessible	2.94 (7)	2.5 (2)	2.62 (Other)	3.25 (3)
Customer Orientated	2.59 (Other)	2.24 (4)	2.14 (3)	2.5 (6)

Source: Research Data, 2010 *Skills not ranked in the top 10 per country are labeled other i.e. other ranking.

A look at country priorities reveals that Kenya places priority on the following three top skills for her HR practitioners; *Effective communicator, Relationship Builder and Decisive*. What is important to note though is that of the four countries in focus, only Kenya prioritises being *decisive* in the top 10 skills. Two other skills are conspicuously missing in the top ten; *Customer orientation* and *driven to deliver*. HR practice in Kenya has developed to the point where the HR professional is fast taking a centre stage in organisations and the clamour for recognition of HR practitioners has already yielded fruit.

HR practice, in Kenya, is quickly taking its rightful place in business and this can be seen by the development that has taken place in the HR professional body. The Institute of Personnel Management (IPM) has evolved in to the Institute of HR Management (IHRM) and commands membership of a majority of the HR practitioners in Kenya. With the professional membership body maturing in providing its members with opportunities to network and improve their general skill level, HR practitioners in Kenya are quite up to date with global trends and expectations of HR professionals.

As a community, Kenya is generally a fast paced and customer oriented country in comparison, for example, with her East African neighbours. With the general consumer and customer population projecting a more demanding posture and a higher expectation of higher standards of service, this has had an impact on the employee environment. This inherent expectation could explain why the two skills of driven to deliver and customer orientation don't make it in the top ten—these skills are almost taken as a given and are really baseline skills for success in the competitive job market in Kenya.

As mentioned earlier, of the four countries, only Kenya had the skill of **decisive** in the top 10 list. Again this is conspicuous and can be explained by a closer look at the state of HR development in Kenya. In a fast paced environment, the need to make correct decisions on the go is highly prized. The stakeholders in Kenya seem to value HR practitioners that can take decisions without spending unnecessarily long periods of time thinking through what could, should or would be done. There seems to be a general dislike for a culture of indecision or 'sweeping issues under the carpet' and HR professionals are called upon to support the business and step up the speed in decision making.

Kenya's colonial history could also have impacted the work ethic in the country and it is common in offices to find practices that can be attributed to the British influence. As an example, the fast pace, drive for results and customer orientated culture could all be attributed to this British influence which resulted in a culture where hard work, persistence and quality work was rewarded.

> *The successful HR professional in Kenya is an **effective communicator** who builds **relationships**, is **personally credible** and demonstrates **decisiveness** in their work. This "HR type" complements the country culture and places the HR practitioner at a vantage position.*

43

Ghana is the only country amongst the four that places **relationship builder** as the top skill effectively replacing **effective communicator** from the top spot. Ghana has a very close knit culture that truly values relationships. The culture is so strong that at times even though a colleague may know of someone who has committed an offence, they would hesitate to "whistle blow" or tell on that person because they would not like to be responsible for the individual losing their job if it could result in such a sanction. Ghana's culture is one of respect for authority and seniority and some behaviours that may be acceptable in other countries such as Kenya or Nigeria could be frowned upon.

In Ghana, talking around issues rather than being blunt and open is the norm which means that to succeed in this culture, a lot of the decision making or influencing will happen outside the formal decision making channels. The formal meeting is only meant to affirm or confirm the decision rather than debate the issues. To succeed in such a culture, networking ability and cultivating strong relationships becomes an absolutely crucial skill.

The skill of **courage to challenge** does not make the top 10 cut in Ghana probably because it runs counter to the culture of respect for seniority and authority levels. A straight forward approach could be taken as an affront depending on the individual being addressed. Decision making tends to be a longer process as a lot of work needs to be done in the background to build allies and convince stakeholders before formal decisions can be taken. For an HR practitioner, ignorance of this "protocol" can hinder success at the work place.

44

Being **accessible** takes the third spot after effective communicator and this is understandable given the priority placed on relationship building. Accessibility is key to building relationships and for HR practitioners in Ghana, there is a need to create forums and avenues to access the various stakeholders in order to build closer work relationships.

> *To be effective as an HR practitioner in Ghana, the HR professional should strive to **build relationships, communicate effectively** and be **accessible**. A challenging approach would cause discomfort and make it harder to foster the relationships necessary to get results at the work place.*

South Africa respondents relegate **relationship builder** to the fifth spot and do not prioritise being **accessible** in the top ten skills. It is almost as if there is a desire to push out anything that could be perceived as building personal relationships at work. In fact the Labour legislation is such that any semblance of favouritism or nepotism could attract very high penalties and this "arms length approach" to work place relationships could actually stem from the legal infrastructure. The top three skill priorities in South Africa are **effective communicator, personally credible and customer orientation**. Given the political past (apartheid regime), a general mistrust in the society amongst different groups of people could easily have transferred to the organisational space and the work place. The desire for open and honest communication and the personal credibility of the communicator are a priority in such a society as there is a need to quickly build and raise the trust levels. This could explain the skill priorities demanded for the HR professional in South Africa.

45

The third ranked skill by South African respondents is **customer orientation**. In the more developed economies, customers tend to take the centre stage and this is no different in South Africa. Amongst the four countries under comparison, South Africa is by far the most developed and the closest to the more developed western economies. In addition, the South African respondent places the skill of **courage to challenge** in the fourth place; the highest amongst all the countries under review. Courage to challenge is an important skill for continuous improvement and especially in situations where it is necessary to bring to the table an alternative perspective.

> *For the HR professional in South Africa remember to hone your skills in **effective communication**, be sure to build and protect your **personal credibility** and bring the **customer perspective** to the fore of the HR strategy.*

For Nigeria, the top three skills for HR professionals are **effective communicator, accessible** and **relationship builder**. Nigeria as a country does have this "larger than life" persona attributed to it mainly driven by the sheer size and population of the country. However from a cultural perspective, Nigerians are quite confident and have a more "in your face" kind of approach - a very direct type of communication.

The priority given to **accessibility** could be attributed to a culture where seniority comes with expectation of certain types of perks—the corner office, a personal assistant, etc and this by itself could be a barrier to free interaction. From the respondent scores on accessibility, Nigeria scores the lowest in this category (2.5) compared to Ghana with the highest (3.25), Kenya with a score of 2.94 and South Africa at 2.62. This would give the impression that given the priority listing by respondents in

Nigeria (second position) stakeholders would like HR professionals to place more emphasis on accessibility.

Courageous to challenge, is not ranked in the top ten skills and for those that are familiar with the Nigerian culture, a challenging approach is almost synonymous with being a Nigerian. Nigerians tend to be quite confident and ready to challenge any decision or direction that they don't understand or agree with. Unlike in Ghana where the society would generally frown at an individual who constantly challenges ideas and initiatives especially when they are fronted by the boss, Nigerian culture embraces this approach. For the skill not to make it to the top ten could be an indicator that it is not perceived as a priority but rather a skill that is a given (non-negotiable).

> *To succeed in Nigeria as an HR professional,* **effective communication, accessibility, relationship building** *and a general aura of* **confidence** *and* **courage to challenge** *would be a good repertoire of skills.*

47

From the analysis above, which explores the impact of country culture on the expectations of HR practitioners, it is evident that as a decision science Human Resource practice could be closer to the Marketing discipline in the sense of "thinking global but acting local". The challenge often posed to HR practitioners is that they should become more like Finance. However, the fact that a particular country culture can have a 'game changing' impact on the skills required for HR practitioners raises some pertinent questions in terms of where HR should focus in its quest to mature as a discipline—Finance or Marketing? Is standardisation, just like International Accounting Standards (IAS), or localisation which is often the approach adopted by Marketing the way to go for HR?

This line of thought about the possible closeness between the fields of Human Resource practice and Marketing will be explored in the final section; the future of Human Resource practice.

Part Three

The State of HR Skill Development

I t is one thing to acknowledge the skills that gain priority listing on the stakeholder maps, to critically examine how HR professionals are currently scored against these skills and totally something else to appreciate how the HR professional is currently being equipped with these skills. For the survey, stakeholders were asked to identify the specific skills, in the immediate short term that they would dedicate finances, time and effort to develop. In addition, the respondents were asked to indicate how HR behavioural skills are currently developed within their organisations.

Priority skill for Development

The stakeholders proposed different skills that they would like HR professionals to up skill in the short term. CEO's indicated that the skill they would like their HR professionals to immediately develop is *Courage to challenge*. This was not surprising given that the score for this skill across all respondents ranked quite low (2.31) and was also ranked amongst the bottom three in terms of current skill level.

51

The HR profession has undergone quite some criticism in this area with a view that HR practitioners tend to play in their court and do not generally contribute during discussions around the P&L (Profit and Loss accounts). The fact that it is not as easy to quantify the contribution of HR into clean and crisp numbers that are totally objective and can be reflected in the company financials has led to a perception that HR is "fluffy" and not bottom line driven. This is not necessarily correct and more than ever before, organisations have endorsed the role of HR in achieving both top line and bottom line results.

The reason given by CEOs for prioritising courage to challenge skill for development is that HR professionals have a view of what is happening on the ground and especially with employees and that this alternative perspective provides a valued dimension that is critical to decision making and for business success and continuity.

HR professionals who take on the role of challenging the business strategy would add the people perspective that is often times left out or relegated in the general discussions in the boardroom. When the HR voice is absent, the employee voice is muted and important people decisions are made from a cost or profit perspective which could work in the short term but could have adverse long term impact.

In addition to developing the skill of **courage to challenge, CEOs** would like HR professionals to further develop the skill of **effective communicator**. Effective communication remains the top skill for the HR professional and it should probably be incorporated as a module in Human Resource training programs.

For the **Line Manager**, the priority skill the HR professionals should develop is **customer orientation**. It is important to note that closely ranked with this priority was **courage to challenge**. Line Managers intimated that HR practitioners tend to forget that employees are the internal customers of HR and that if the internal customer is not satisfied, the external customer does not get the best possible service.

Line Managers would like HR to listen more, be flexible and take the view of the employee forward when strategic decisions are being made or when policies are being designed. Line Managers suggest that aligning the internal and external customers is one thing HR could do to have positive impact on the organisation's bottom line. Such alignment would lead to better internal customer experience which would in turn impact the external customer experience. A satisfied employee may not directly translate to a satisfied external customer but a dissatisfied employee is highly likely to generate low customer satisfaction as reflected in satisfaction ratings or customer loyalty scores.

HR professionals ranked **Visionary** skills at the top of the development list due to a need to ensure focus on the future of the organisation and not just the short term. When developing employee capability and the talent pipeline, it is important not to just focus on current needs but to also start building the capabilities needed by the organisation for future success.

In addition, with HR professionals having taken a place in the board room, the need to contribute to general business discussions calls for visionary skills. It was also indicated from the survey results that in order to effectively partner the CEO, whose horizon is normally three to five years or longer, the HR professional is expected to demonstrate a similar thinking horizon.

53

The other skill identified by HR professionals as a priority for development was **skilled influencer**. HR professionals work with a multiple range of stakeholders. Especially in times of introducing and managing change, HR has to carry along these stakeholders and a need to influence them and achieve win/win situations becomes critical. An HR professional who is a skilled influencer will drive the HR agenda without necessarily having to deal with large amounts of resistance to change. The need to work with Unions and balance their demands with management priorities requires HR professionals to master the skill of influencing. As a skilled influencer, the HR professional can build allies long before there is a need to call on them for support and therefore reduce the time it takes to build consensus and momentum behind desired changes.

Country perspective on skill development

The country perspective on the priorities for skill development provides an additional dimension that is valuable. In **Nigeria** for example, the top skill identified for the HR professional to develop is **Courage to challenge** whereas in **Ghana, customer orientation** is prioritised. For **South Africa, driven to deliver** is prioritised whereas in **Kenya**, the need to develop **visionary skills** is flagged up.

Respondents provided a variety of reasons for selecting the priority skill for development. In **Nigeria,** the survey results indicated that HR professionals tend to follow management decisions without necessarily bringing to the attention of decision makers the people perspective. Examples given to support this view included redundancy decisions taken in a rush and resulting in having to hire replacements to take on the same roles at a higher salary as well as the employment of expatriates even when local skills were available. These were cited as indicators that HR does not have the courage to challenge even when it is clear that the preferred management decision is not the right one for the business. HR professionals are being called upon to effectively play the role of the organisational conscience and guard the organisation against actions that go against organisational values, mission and vision.

In **South Africa**, the respondents present HR professionals as more laid back and give the view that there is a low sense of urgency in the profession. This is given as the reason for wanting HR professionals to develop the skill of driven to deliver. As HR supports customer facing functions that have tight delivery timelines, the same tempo is recommended for HR in order to speed up decisions and provide the support needed by the other internal customers. Coupled with the fact that customer orientation is identified as a priority skill for HR practitioners, a low score under the skill of driven to deliver, would generally slow down the business in its response to market demands. That sense of urgency is currently felt to be lacking within the HR practitioners.

In **Ghana**, customer orientation is identified as the top skill to be developed by HR professionals. Of interest here is that the reasons given for wanting HR professionals to be customer oriented are very similar to those given by South Africa respondents under driven to deliver. Respondents felt that HR needs to speed up responses to employee queries so the final customer can get served faster. There was also a sense that once the HR function, as the custodian of the company culture, was customer oriented the likelihood that other functions would also focus on the customer would be high as HR would have helped build a customer centric culture in the organisation.

Kenyan respondents identified being visionary as the top skill HR professionals should develop. The reasons for this include a need to take on a leadership role in the organisation therefore calling for visionary skills. In addition, the need to partner the CEO in the ever changing organisational landscape calls for the need for HR to adopt a futuristic approach in the design of HR strategy, work culture and environment.

Comparative table - Skill to Develop vs priority Skill for Success

Respondent/Country	Priority Level	Priority Skill needed for Success
Line manager	Customer Orientation	Effective Communicator
CEO	Courage to Challenge	Effective Communicator
HR Professional	Visionary	Effective Communicator
Kenya	Skilled Influencer	Effective Communicator
Ghana	Customer Orientation	Relationship Builder
Nigeria	Courage to Challenge	Effective Communicator
South Africa	Driven to Deliver	Effective Communicator

Source: Research Data, 2010

The trend amongst all the respondents was to select a skill for immediate development where HR had a really low score rather than investing in a skill that is currently listed as a priority for success. This approach tends to be a common approach to skill development although it is not necessarily the most effective method for getting immediate improvement. None of the respondents prioritised any of the top three skills (effective communicator, relationship builder and personally credible) they identified for the success of HR professionals for immediate development.

The desire to fix weakness rather than develop the most critical skills could lead to a delay in the up skilling of HR professionals in the areas that would immediately impact business results. Given that there is always a scarcity of time and resources, the option to concentrate development on the top skills for success is one that organisations should consider as they design the development agenda for HR practitioners.

Skill Development Options

57

Respondents were asked to select from a list of skill development options, the methods that were prevalent in their organisation. The overall results of the survey across all respondents prioritised three methods as the most commonly used to develop HR behavioural skills; *on the job exposure (76.7%), external training (64.1%) and tailored internal training (55.1%).*

The list of development options is provided below:

Skill Development options

Options	Options
On the Job Exposure	Participation in Communities of Practice
Executive Coaching	Scheduled Experience Sharing Sessions
Professional Body Membership	Online experiential training programs
External Training Programs	Webinars
Tailored Internal Training programs	Targeted CEO Coaching Sessions
Short Term Assignments to another function	360 degree feedback programs
Formal Mentoring Program	Membership to key committees
Job Rotation Programs	

Source: Research Data, 2010

Any of the development options can be utilised to support behaviour change but with differing ease of implementation and success levels.

On the job exposure

This is probably the most common method employed for skill development. It is a very effective method if it is purposefully implemented. However, more often than not, with this method, individuals are left to their own designs and initiative to pick up learning and apply it on the job. Unless the line manager is more hands on and involved in day to day team development, the success of this method tends to be directly linked to an individual's affinity to self learning and initiative.

Although it is a cost effective and practical method of development that ensures immediate transfer of learning, without good direction the individual could end up learning behaviours that could be negative and would need unlearning in the future. Also because this development method tends to be unstructured, the quality of learning may not be at the level desired by the business. From research data, this method of development was identified as the most frequently used to develop HR professionals.

Executive Coaching

In the past, coaching was associated with poor performers in the sense that it is those that proved to be performing below expectations that got assigned a coach, often as a last resort before disengagement. This has totally flipped to a point now where having a coach is almost viewed as a measure of success. High potential candidates and those with promising careers in organisations are the ones the business is willing to spend coaching money on.

This development approach is quite expensive but is absolutely invaluable. The benefits gained from having a coach especially one from outside the business include the objectivity that an outside coach brings to the coaching relationship with a goal to support the individual to develop. The external perspective that the coach brings tends to add value beyond the initial goal of the coaching engagement.

In Africa, the concept of executive coaching is fast picking up though there is a general shortage of trained coaches in the continent and as mentioned earlier, the costs are still quite prohibitive therefore limiting the number of organisations that invest in executive coaching.

Professional Body Membership

Joining professional bodies is an effective method of development for both starters and seasoned professionals. Most professional associations offer accreditation training and ongoing skill development opportunities for its members. In addition, belonging to a professional body often offers networking opportunities that allow ongoing knowledge and best practice sharing.

60

Some professional bodies also enforce codes of conduct that ensure that the practitioners adhere to strict standards of performance therefore raising the general professionalism of members. The advantages of professional body membership are many but key amongst them is the speed at which one can borrow great practices from colleagues and tailor them for implementation in their own organisation.

External Training Programs

A lot of the behaviour skill development within HR is still very reliant on external training programs. This is where open programs on a specific skill e.g. 'developing influencing skills' are publicised for interested individuals from a variety of organisations to subscribe to. This method offers certain advantages including cost effectiveness. Such programs also offer opportunities for networking and learning from practitioners in other organisations.

The disadvantages of external programs include the fact that the individual learning needs or gaps may not be fully addressed as the programs tend to be generic in order to appeal to a wide range of participants. The curriculum design may not address specific skill gaps needed to handle organisational challenges and as such the program effectiveness could be compromised.

Tailored Internal Development Programs

At times, organisations design and deliver tailored programs for their practitioners. The advantage of using this approach is that the information and skills covered in the program are specific to the organisation and can lead to a better transfer of knowledge to the work place. Real work scenarios and case studies can be incorporated in such programs making them very practical for the delegates.

61

Tailored programs can be quite expensive as training providers have to spend time creating specific curriculum for each program. The lead time to design and deliver such programs may also be lengthy affecting the frequency of course delivery. That said, tailored programs are very effective at addressing specific needs identified through learning needs assessments.

Short Term Assignments to other Functions

Within the Human Resource profession, it is not very common for practitioners to be seconded to other parts of the business for development purposes. Short term assignments provide deep insight in to business requirements that can trigger a fresh approach to the way HR adds value to the organisation. A three months stint in Sales, for example, would create a high level of awareness for the HR practitioner to experience firsthand the challenges faced by the sales force in terms of resources or administrative bureaucracies. A deep understanding of what it takes to generate revenue brings HR professionals much closer to the business.

With such understanding, the HR professional can review policies, processes and procedures to empower the business to focus on delivering results. Resourcing, reward or even training policies and procedures can be tailored to the specific needs of the business once HR practitioners have a better understanding of business needs.

Formal Mentoring

Unlike coaching, mentoring provides opportunities to learn from the experiences of others that have already succeeded in similar circumstances. This method is quite effective because the practitioner can avoid mistakes and learn from the successes of the mentor.

Finding mentors that have the time to dedicate to up skilling practitioners could be a challenge especially when the relationship has to be formalised. In some organisations, mentoring programs are institutionalised such that senior managers are expected to mentor younger managers as part of their own leadership development.

Although this method of development is quite effective, the time demand required of the mentor to engage in formal mentoring relationship does act as a barrier to the number of professionals that benefit from this development option.

Job Rotation

Job rotation, as a development option, helps individuals experience a different job and often learn and make use of a new set of competencies. Job rotation often leads to the introduction of new ideas, new processes and often scrapping of processes that don't add value. Job rotation especially within the same function provides an opportunity to learn new skills in a "safe" environment where the previous role holder is accessible to provide ongoing guidance.

The exposure provided by job rotation options also leads to the development of new behavioural skills as each job holder tends to interact in a different way with stakeholders.

63

Participation in Communities of Practice

Communities of practice offer individuals the opportunity to keep up with developments within a profession. Members of such communities come together and discuss specific challenges they face in their profession or explore creative ways of handling issues within their profession.

This could take the form of one of the practitioners researching a topic and making a presentation to the team or inviting a leading specialist in a specific area of practice to provide insights and guidance on issues of interest to the group. Communities of practice are a very effective way of raising the standards of practice while using fairly informal methods. The networking advantage that results from participating in a community of practice provides additional opportunities to develop and grow.

Scheduled experience sharing sessions

These involve getting an individual who has successfully implemented a project or attended a specific training programs to share their experience and learning with others. This development option, though not often utilized, provides a forum for sharing best practices and this could spur innovation and continuous improvement in an organisation.

Often times, due to cost or other considerations, only one individual gets to attend a training that could be beneficial to a number of other people in the team. Experience sharing provides a forum to share such learning and to answer questions that other team members may have and spreads knowledge in the organisation without having to incur huge training expenses. If such experience sharing sessions are successfully used the impact can be quite positive and significant.

Online Experiential programs

Such programs are available on the internet but unlike other online courses, they offer the opportunity to test ones learning.

An example could be facilitation training, where case studies are provided as part of the training and the individual has to accurately respond to questions, scenarios and case studies in order to proceed with the training. The design of the training is such that the trainee has to carry out some assignments and get feedback as to why their response is the right or wrong answer in order to proceed.

This ensures an instant transfer of learning through immediate feedback and an opportunity to practice the newly acquired skills.

Webinars

Webinars are online sessions where leading experts and specialists in a field of expertise share their knowledge to a virtual audience. The participants need to log in or dial in to participate. There are many advantages of participating in webinars as they provide access to top notch facilitators without having to travel to distant venues. For transnational audiences, webinars are a perfect development option.

Another advantage of using webinars is that the latest information, innovation or discovery on a specific topic can be accessed from any part of the world. For some webinars, attendees have an opportunity to pose questions in advance for the webinar organisers to respond to during the session which adds to the effectiveness of this development method.

Targeted CEO coaching session

By the nature of their job, CEOs have a view of organisations that is unique and quite valuable for upcoming executives. A coaching session with the CEO can provide insights that could prove invaluable to the coachee. Indeed, having the CEO as a coach also tends to open career doors and is a great networking opportunity.

The outcome of such coaching could lead to gaining much needed visibility in an organisation; often a necessity for accelerated career growth. The access that is provided by such coaching sessions could also lead to a better understanding of what opportunities may be coming up in the future and how to position oneself to benefit from such opportunities.

Though rare, CEO coaching sessions can make all the difference in growing and retaining the top talent in an organisation.

360 Degree Feedback

66

360 degree feedback is probably the most effective way of raising self awareness and identifying an individual's strengths and areas of weakness. This approach provides an all round view from key stakeholders—self assessment, line manager, peers, direct reports and any others as may be appropriate (customers, clients).

The key to successful use of 360 degree feedback is in how the face to face feedback is carried out and how such feedback is used to support development. It is always useful to approach a 360 degree feedback process with an open mind and a desire to improve. The confidential nature of the 360 degree feedback process normally leads to quite an objective view of an individual that may not be easily accessed or diagnosed through the use of other development options.

Membership to key committees

Serving in specific committees can provide an individual with great experiences and exposure for development. Serving in the executive committee for example provides a unique view of the organisations from all angles and affords the individual with the opportunity to get a feel of what the priorities of shareholders and senior management are.

Apart from the executive committee, other committees such as a culture change committee, a vision cascade committee, a recognition committee and other such committees also provide opportunities for learning new skills.

Skill Development Survey Results

67

As discussed earlier, the overall results from the survey indicate that the most commonly used method for developing behavioural skills is **on the job exposure** with a score of 76.7%. This is followed by **external training program**s and **tailored internal training programs** with scores of 64.1% and 55.1% respectively.

HR Competence Development Options

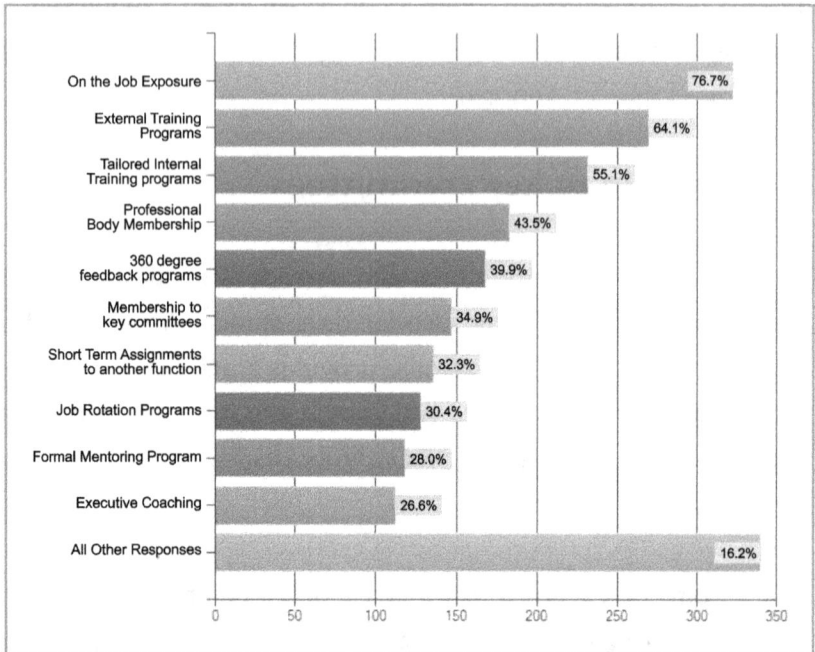

Source: Research Data, 2010

The research gives an insight in to the state of HR professional development in each country. **South Africa** is quite advanced in terms of HR development as revealed in the survey data. South Africa's list for skill development stands out in that an overwhelming 82% of respondents indicate **360 degree programmes** as the top development method followed by **on the job exposure 69%** and **tailored internal training programmes** at 69%.

This differs from all other countries that had on the job exposure taking precedence over external programs and internal tailored programs. Often times when on-the-job development is the primary skill development option, it should be coupled with baseline skill assessment and on the job coaching. Without these additional aspects, skill development could be haphazard, unstructured and generally left to the initiative of the job holder. The fact that on the job training is the priority option in **Ghana, Nigeria and Kenya** could be an indicator of the lack of structured HR skill development in these countries.

Effective Skill Development

Across all the respondent types (line manager, CEO, HR professional) and countries, the respondents indicated that the most appropriate method to develop behavioural skills was through the use of **feedback and coaching**. This response by survey participants differs from the current skill development options currently in use in all the countries, apart from South Africa. The behavioural feedback provided from 360 degree programmes increases the level of self awareness and allows the HR professional to map a tailored development plan that can take them to a higher behavioural competence level. When such feedback is coupled with on the job coaching, the possibility that the skill competency level will be progressively increased is much higher as compared to reliance on picking up skills as one goes along.

The combination of feedback and coaching as part of a development plan is referred to as **"deliberate practice"** (Zenger & Folkman, 2002). This is an extremely effective skill development approach that is used in the field of sports. Sports trainers understand that to develop a skill, there is a need to identify the starting point (a baseline assessment), come up with

69

a training plan and work with a coach to adjust behaviour until the target skill level is reached. This approach can also be mirrored in behaviour skill development.

So how does an HR practitioner improve on their soft skill levels? The next section provides a toolbox for this.

Part Four

Behavioural Skill Development Guide

This section seeks to put together a quick guide for HR Behavioural skill development. The guide is not exhaustive and should be used in conjunction with other skill development options that may be within the reach of each HR professional. For each of the behaviour skills, the skill development guide is composed of:

a)   A short definition of the skill.
b)   Some indicators of the skill at work to help identify whether an HR professional uses the skill.
c)   Some tips for quick skill improvement - this serves as a quick "cheat sheet" that HR professionals can make a reference to in order to fast track skill development.
d)   A cluster of other skills that are related to a specific behavioural skill. A positive improvement in any of these other skills in the cluster has a positive impact on performance in the specific skill being developed.
e)   Reference to a book that an HR professional can read to get some more indepth knowledge of the skill in reference.

Effective Communicator

This is the ability to give clear messages or information using a variety of medium (oral or written) whilst appreciating the needs of the audience.

Behavioural Indicators	Quick Tips For Skill Development
Personalizes messages so as to connect to the audience	Understand the audience - what is appropriate for one audience may be totally inappropriate for a different one. Identify what is critically important for them and make reference to this in your message.
Conveys a vision - focuses on the shared or common aspects of the communication and references the past and the familiar to woo the audience	Think through what you hope to gain from the communication. What would a successful outcome of this communication look like?
Acknowledges any sticky or thorny issues that exist rather than pretending that they don't exist	Consider possible objections and come up with credible responses. This is useful for both written and oral communication.
Persuades - elicits nods by sequencing ideas and getting "yes" responses from audience	Make linkages to previous communications if relevant to increase credibility and believability. Get the audience nodding and also practice your communication beforehand.
Drives the point home by emphasizing the key aspects of the message that the audience needs to take home	Emphasize the 2 or 3 things that the audience ought to recall and repeat this in the summary of your message.
Makes effective use of homour	Be careful to choose homour that is acceptable to your audience. If you are not sure whether a joke is appropriate, do not make use of it.
Has the ability to use anaecdotes and stories to drive their point home	Come up with an outline plan for the communication including a strong opening, a persuasive middle and a memorable closing. This is the essence of great story telling - context, some drama and a climax.

Skills that have a high positive impact on the ability to be an *effective communicator* include:

▶ **Personal credibility** - the trust that comes with this skill paves the way for effective communication. When an individual is perceived to be credible, the audience is more receptive to the message. Lack of credibility can lead to a distortion of an otherwise great message.

▶ **Confident** - a confident person exudes an aura of self assurance that comes from having a good grasp of their subject. When communicating, presenting a confident posture increases the ability to be believed.

▶ **Enthusiasm** - this helps inject passion in communication increasing the ability to woo and influence people. Communicating a message in flat monotone or without passion leads to reduced energy and interest in the subject of communication.

▶ **Creativity** - this makes the message catchy and easy to remember. In today's work place, there are loads of messages that need to be communicated and only the memorable messages will be remembered. Using a story, analogy or a different way of passing a message improves memorability.

▶ **Multiple perspectives** - helps with acknowledging different stakeholder interests in the communication. Usually, the same communication is made to a group of people that have differing interests. Taking account of this and ensuring that there is something in the generic

75

communication that appeals to multiple stakeholders will ensure their perspective is incorporated in the message.

Supporting Skills for Effective Communicator

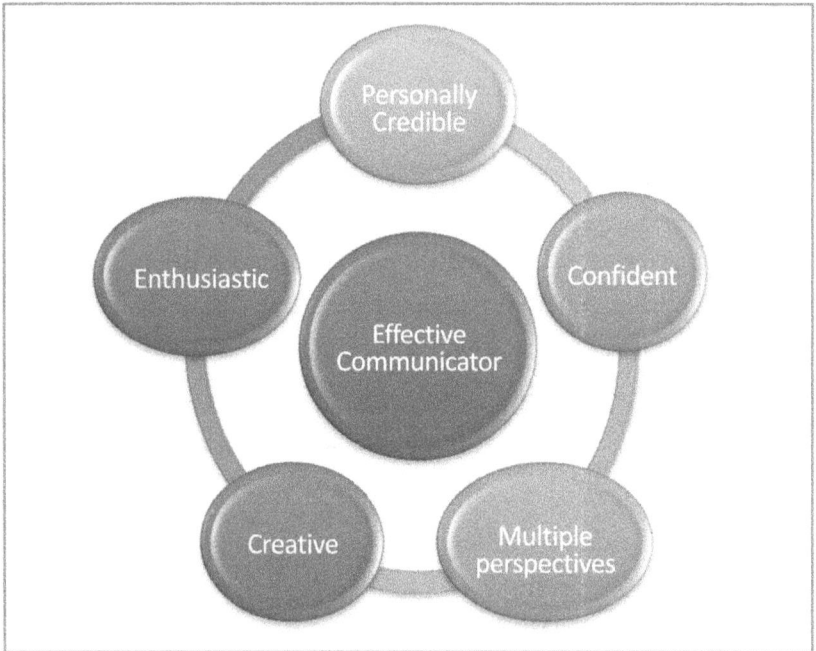

Book resource: *The art and science of communication: Tools for effective communication in the workplace (2008). By P.S. Perkins and Les Brown.*

Relationship Building

This is the ability to identify, develop, nurture and maintain productive interactions with key stakeholders.

Behavioural Indicators	Quick Tips For Skill Development
An effective listener	Listen to understand and not just to respond. Ask for clarifications, paraphrase what has been said and summarize to get absolute clarity. Give full attention by maintaining eye contact and being a participant in the communication - don't just be dead silent.
Seeks to understand other people's point of view	Talk to people informally and ask for their opinions and views on a variety of issues. This is important prior to meetings where your goal is to get a certain decision.
Is friendly, open and receptive to other people	Greet people rather than passing them along without acknowledging them. When you meet people, give them a genuine complement as early in the interaction as possible.
Takes account of the other party's interests	Have an interest in people and find out about what they value - family, a hobby, etc before delving in to areas of your own interests. Consider compromise in certain areas and aim for decisions that lead to win/win outcomes.
Reaches out to others rather than being aloof	Participate in informal gatherings and events and be part of the community. Walk around and meet people and don't just wait for them to come to you.
Handles criticism tactfully	Acknowledge feedback given and accept it as an indicator that better clarity, communication or interaction could help change the perception. If criticism is accurate, work on improvement but always acknowledge feedback.

Skills that have a high positive impact on the ability to **build relationships** include:

▶ **Reward & Recognition** - acknowledging the contribution of the other party is a sign of approval and improves the bond in relationships. Reward is a great way of reinforcing the behaviour or a desired outcome.

▶ **Integrity** - an ethical person that maintains confidences is a people magnet and this makes it easy to build relationships. Integrity is really the core of every relationship and fosters trust which speeds up decision making.

▶ **Networking** - the skill of networking calls for initiative from an individual to proactively keep relationships alive and to look for areas of interest and connection with others.

▶ **Effective communication** - communicating effectively is likely to gain followership and loyalty from others and build relationships. Effective communication also ensures that all the parties involved feel heard and can share their points of view.

▶ **Inclusive** - a person who practices inclusivity acknowledges the differences in people and rather than discriminating on the basis of differences, acknowledges the differences and highlights unique contributions that emanate from these differences.

Supporting Skills for Relationship Builder

Book resource: *The seven steps to successful relationships (a practical guide for everyone). (2005). By Keith & Maura Leon*

Personally Credible

This is the degree of "believability" or the degree of being thought of as trustworthy.

Behavioural Indicators	Quick Tips For Skill Development
A good track record of delivering work results	An achiever gathers a reputation that leads to amassing credibility. People that have proven ability to deliver on their previous promises are likely to have a high believability factor.
Considered a role model	Confront difficult issues and push for resolution. Don't demand from others what you would not do if you were in their shoes.
Having ethics at the centre of one's dealings	Stand up for what you believe in and speak up as appropriate even when you are the lone voice with that point of view.
Delivers on one's promises	Don't promise what you can't deliver. Go the extra mile to meet your deliverables as it adds to your credibility.
Honest in one's dealings	Be truthful and don't evade questions because the answers may not be what the audience hopes to hear. Explain why the answer is "no" instead of just rejecting proposals.
Ability to follow through	Share information in a timely manner to avoid surprises for your stakeholders. Don't just follow up (to know the status) but follow through (to complete the assignment).

Skills that have a high positive impact on the ability to be *personally credible* include:

▶ **Honouring Confidences** - people that can keep confidences elicit trust and are perceived as being people of integrity. Spreading or sharing information that has been passed in confidence is a sure way of reducing an individual's personal credibility.

▶ **Authentic** - this means that there is congruence between what one says and what they do. This builds an individual's credibility factor and believability level. Authentic people are true to their character and tend to be easy to trust.

▶ **Competent** - a competent person is more credible when they speak or advocate an action within their technical remit. Presenting a proposal in an area of competence is likely to be convincing to an audience.

▶ **Keeping Commitments** - this provides the currency for future trust and confirms to stakeholders that the individual is one that keeps their word. Making promises and not keeping them is a sure way of breaking trust and credibility making it more difficult to be believed in the future.

▶ **Valuing others** - when people feel valued and appreciated, they gain the sense that the other party is a "good person" and this increases the level of credibility. People like to be around friends and those that respect them.

Supporting Skills for Personally Credible

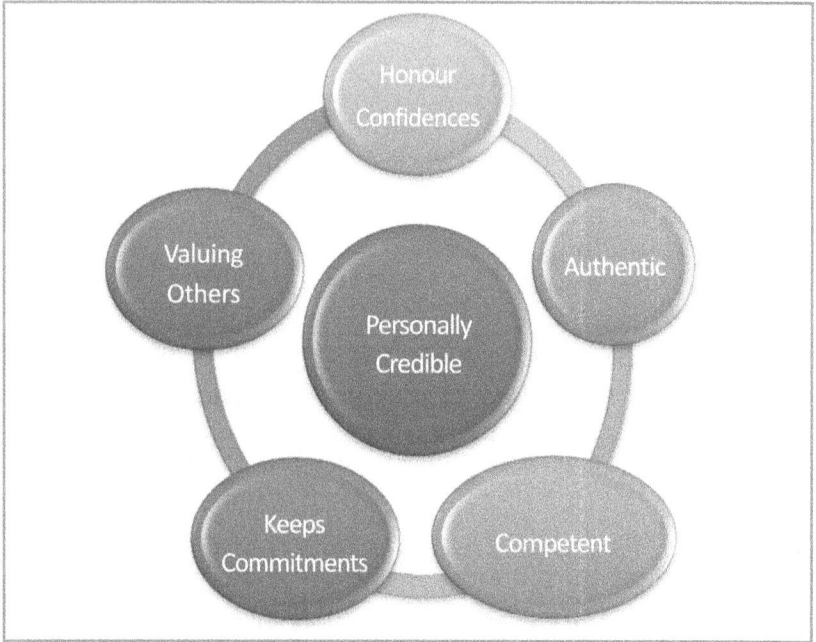

Book Resource: *The Personal Credibility Factor: how to get it, keep it and get it back (if you've lost it) (2009). By Sandy Allgeier,*

Skilled Influencer

The ability to convince others to follow a particular course of action.

Behavioural Indicators	Quick Tips For Skill Development
Adopts a convincing approach	Use stories to convince and elicit hope. Give examples and provide testimonials of where the proposed action has worked before and how it worked. Elicit the support of others that have credibility in the eyes of the people you need to convince.
Highlights the areas of common ground	Research the issue at hand and hold informal conversations to understand areas of shared interests as well as areas that may be thorny. Come up with fall back options in case of barriers in reaching consensus.
Points out the down sides of a proposal and demonstrates how these will be mitigated	Think through the pros and cons of any proposal from all perspectives. This will help in coming up with fall back positions if required.
Communicates openly and is not seen as having a hidden agenda	Adopting an approach of sharing information openly and influencing from a point of good faith will accelerate consensus building and decision making
Carries the other party along	Identify what is important to the other party and link this to own point of view or proposal. The ability to prove that by reaching a certain decision, the interests of all parties will be achieved is a great tactic.
Elicits trust from others	Suggest a pilot, trial or experiential learning if the change required is big. This gives the other party an opportunity to trial on a small scale what is being advocated before taking a full decision.
Celebrates wins	Identifies quick wins and looks for every opportunity to celebrate together. Celebrating wins helps increase team bonds and raise the level of motivation.

Skills that have a high positive impact on the ability to *influence* include:

▶ **Motivating others** - when stakeholders can connect with "what is in it for me" in a project or initiative, they are more likely to be influenced to participate. Motivating people by painting a picture of what could be will influence them to want to be part of the future.

▶ **Connecting to the inner good** - a skilled influencer will go beyond what look like challenges or barriers and connect to the inner good in the audience being influenced. This could be the desire to participate in an activity that has long term impact or that benefits communities.

▶ **Offer trial or personal experience** - trial increases the ability of adoption for any change process and explains why new product development adopts pilots and product trials. Trial and experience creates a connection that helps influence people.

▶ **Peer pressure** - peer pressure can be positively used to make it "unattractive" to behave in certain ways and is possibly one of the most effective ways of changing behaviour.

▶ **Honour Choice** - acknowledging that individual's have options is an effective way of influencing. The choices could include "no action" and that is a choice that an individual can make. It is important to make clear the consequences of the various options though.

Supporting Skills for Skilled Influencer

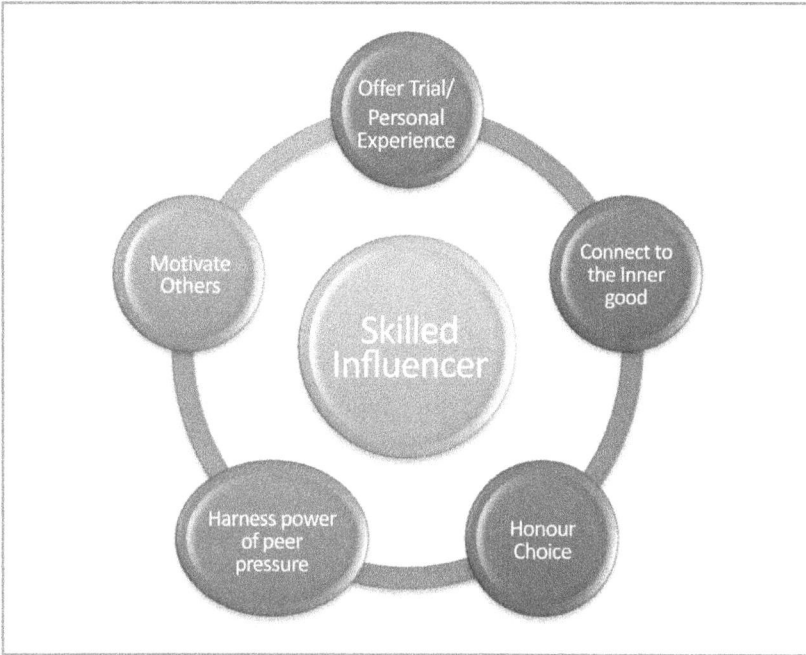

Book Resource: *Influencer: The power to change anything (2008). By Kerry Patterson, Joseph Grenny, David Maxfield, Ron Macmillan and Al Switzler,*

Decisive

The ability to exercise good judgment and make sound decisions.

Behavioural Indicators	Quick Tips For Skill Development
Knows when to make the decision and when to consult	There are several levels of proactivity and these indicate the level of independence one has in making decisions. Sometimes the right thing is to take action whereas other circumstances may call for you to seek advice or to seek permission to take action.
Weighs the risks in the process of decision making	Use decision tools such as SWOT analysis, benefits and weaknesses analysis, fish bone, mind maps and brainstorming to clearly identify the risks in a decision and speed up decision making.
Proactively communicates decisions taken rather than waiting for others to demand for a decision	Give a decision even if it is "wait" or "not now" rather than just waiting until the final point to say "yes" or "no".
Time taken to make decisions is commensurate with the kind of decision being taken	Keep track of precedents and previous decisions made in similar circumstances as well as policies that may guide decision making. Having such information at hand speeds up decisions such that only new situations or additional complexities need to be investigated.
Pushes for decisions at interim points and not just the final decision	Decision making is more of a process rather than an event. Identifying points in the process where one can push for a decision allows for faster and smoother decision making.
Understands the impact of indecision	Look at the bigger picture in analyzing situations to weigh the impact of indecision. In an emergency situation, it can be fatal to decide to call a focus group to deliberate on an issue.

Skills that have a high positive impact on the ability to be **decisive** include:

▶ **Planning and organizing** - people that are better at planning make decisions faster as they can access the necessary information needed to evaluate options. Keeping good records and knowing where to access the information e.g. policies will speed up decision making.

▶ **Follow through** - Following through not just following up is the ability to persistently pursue closure of an issue to its conclusion. Those that tend to follow through are perceived to be more decisive.

▶ **Accountable** - Individuals thought to be accountable take responsibility and ownership for projects and outcomes and are therefore more likely to be decisive.

▶ **Disciplined reflection** - this is the art of reflecting on decisions to better understand what worked and what did not. This discipline builds an individual's ability to make faster decisions.

▶ **Nurtures Relationships** - people that have build relationships have the trust of stakeholders and do not need long periods of convincing people to follow a course of action. Covey (2006) refers to it as the "speed of trust" due to the ability to speed up business decisions.

Supporting Skills for being Decisiveness

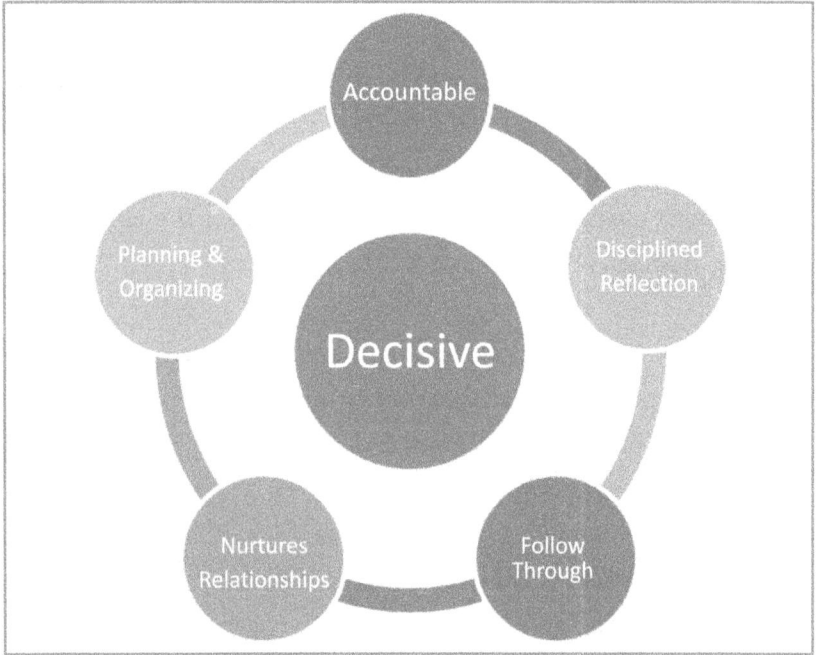

Book resource: *Brilliant Decision Making: what the best decision makers know, do and say (2010). By Robbie Steinhouse*

Customer Orientation

The ability to pick out customer insights, anticipate the needs of the customer and design processes that are geared at satisfying customer needs

Behavioural Indicators for Customer Orientation	Quick Tips For Skill Development
Places oneself in the shoes of the customer. Empathizes with the customer	Empathy is a skill that is paramount in customer service. Being genuinely interested in customer feedback and listening with an intent to resolve any problem, demonstrating understanding and using a language that gives the customer reassurance.
Listens to the needs of the customer	Act on customer feedback and communicate action taken linking it directly to the feedback from the customer. This leads to the customer feeling that he has "been heard". Invites customers to participate in product research and testing.
Works backwards from customer expectations to determine what needs to be done to meet those expectations	Work with the end in mind. Determine the steps needed to achieve the final result. Place milestones and timelines against the goals to make it easy to track progress.
Solicits feedback from customers	Organize customer focus groups and use other forums to get feedback from customers and benchmark these against competitor scores. Carry out blind surveys to determine actual customer loyalty and use this feedback to improve on customer service.
Interprets customers feedback in to insights that can be used to create services or products	Discerning the insight in customer feedback is crucial in coming up with the appropriate response. Insight is derived from linking feedback to a need.
Goes out of the way to meet customer needs	Go the extra mile to meet customer needs and come up with solutions that "wow" the customer lead to increased customer loyalty and retention.

Skills that have a high positive impact on the ability to be *customer orientated* include:

▶ **Problem Solving** - an individual who is good at problem solving is a great asset in a customer service role and follows through customer complaints to resolve them and ensures customer requests are met.

▶ **Insight and Understanding** - the ability to glean insights and get understanding from customer interactions ensures that solutions that are crafted address the customer need. It may not be easy to pick out insights from customer feedback but this is the key to customer satisfaction.

▶ **Relevant** - remaining relevant in terms of service or product offering is what keeps customers engaged and loyal. Without maintaining relevance, there is no attraction from customers to patronise your products or services.

▶ **Results Orientated** - a drive for results is great for customer service as it confirms to customers that someone is putting the effort to meet their needs. When it comes to customers, going the extra mile to meet and exceed their expectations is what keeps them loyal.

▶ **Innovation** - this calls for keeping up with customer needs both current and future and offering services or products that meet and exceed their needs. Delighting customers and creating a WOW experience is great and continuous innovation can keep customers curious about what to expect next.

Supporting Skills for Customer Orientation

Book resource: *Moments of Truth: New Strategies for Today's Customer Driven Economy (1987). By Jan Carlzon*

Courage to Challenge

This is the ability to do the right thing when one is under pressure to do a different thing.

Behavioural Indicators	Quick Tips For Skill Development
Appropriately challenges decisions that are not aligned to the vision, strategy or values of the organisation	Understand the business and what the priorities are to support effective challenging. Getting known as the conscience of the organisation due to the questions you ask makes you more valuable.
Is not shy to give their own opinion and point of view even if it is a lone voice	Create a track record of delivering on results and keeping promises to "earn" the right to challenge. Anyone can challenge but those with credibility get the benefit of doubt even when they are not well prepared to challenge.
Is assertive while maintaining professionalism	Learn to ask powerful questions - questions that have the ability to change the course of things. Keep a note of questions that solicit very good responses. Build relationships as this assures that challenges questions are not interpreted as personal attacks.
Knows when to challenge	Observe people in your organisation that are good at challenging and mirror their behaviours especially how they do it. Do they tend to be direct or they give a pros and cons review before challenging? Organisational culture is key to knowing when to challenge.
Understands context of the issue at hand and appreciated different points of view	Get a coach or a mentor to help you develop this skill. This could be a colleague who watches your behaviour during meetings and provides you feedback on opportunities that you could have used to challenge. The skill grows with time and needs to be practiced.

Skills that have a high positive impact on the ability to have the *courage to challenge* include:

▶ **Business Knowledge** - understanding the business, the challenges both internal and external is a good basis for challenging the strategy, execution or even relevance of initiatives.

▶ **Competent** - a competent person would have a track record of delivering results and this provides the credibility to challenge business direction. It is a lot easier to challenge business decisions if a person is achieving results in their own work area.

▶ **Analytical/Logical** - A logical approach ensures that whatever challenge an individual poses is well thought through and is unlikely to just be brushed aside. A logical approach to posing challenges and questions gives an impression of seriousness and demands a serious response.

93

▶ **Asking questions** - questions have the ability to completely change the direction of things and knowing when to ask questions or the type of questions to ask is a skill that is key for anyone looking to influence business direction.

▶ **Taking calculated risks** - people that take risks are not shy of "rocking the boat" and challenging the status quo. The approach of asking "what is the worst that can happen" provides the courage to advance one's view.

Supporting Skills for Courage to Challenge

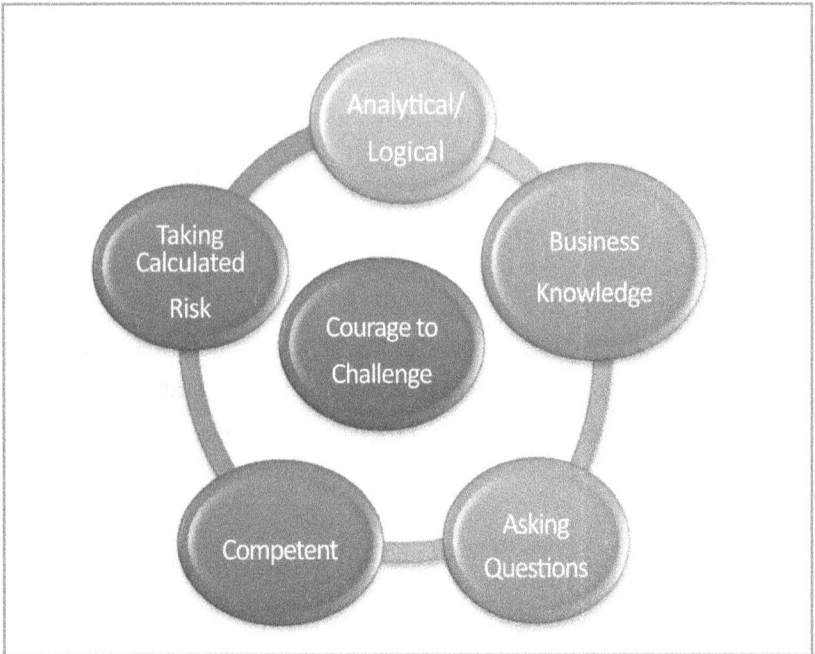

Book resource: *Conscious Courage: Turning every day Challenges into Opportunities (2004). By Maureen Stearns*

Accessible

The ability to be approachable, preferring face to face communication and demonstrating humility.

Behavioural Indicators	Quick Tips For Skill Development
Operates an open door policy	Invite others over and don't just wait for people to come to you. An open door policy is not just an open door. It is more than this and includes how people are treated once in your office.
Is approachable and emits the body language to support this	Get involved in social events that come up at the work place and not just the formal activities. Effectively participate in making the organisation a "family".
Has an inclusive approach	Take time to find out what issues people have and proactively take action to be supportive. Open up to feedback and informal interactions with colleagues. When coming up with new initiatives include a cross section of people in brainstorming sessions or other activities to make them feel part of the final outcome.
Smiles at people	Smiling is a disarming gesture and helps calm and reassure people. Learn to practice your smile - a smile where no teeth show is viewed with distrust. Smile from the heart and in front of the mirror until you are comfortable with the smile as it is probably the first image people will have of you.
Provides opportunities to be accessible and is available	Create the time to be accessible - set aside a time to walk around and meet people for opportunities to forums and sessions.

95

Skills that have a high positive impact on the ability on being **accessible** include:

▶ **Warm smile -** a smile is a very effective tool for displaying a welcome disposition. Smiles are effective to open doors to relationships and lead to conversations even with strangers.

▶ **Positive Optimism -** remaining positive is a good way of remaining accessible. People that are pessimistic or perennial complainers tend to repel people. To become a people magnet, remain positive and allow the energy that flows from being optimistic to pull people to you.

▶ **Flexible -** a flexible person is viewed as accessible. This is because the individual is viewed as able to adopt feedback and change actions on the basis of the views of others.

▶ **A good listener -** a good listener can be said to be a real "people person". When people are listened to, even if their request is not honoured, they feel valued and are drawn to those that listen to them.

▶ **Open minded -** the ability to keep an open mind rather than adopt the stand "my way or the highway" is one that makes an individual more accessible. A physical open door policy is not as important as an open mind and a willingness to consider new information.

Supporting Skills for Accessible

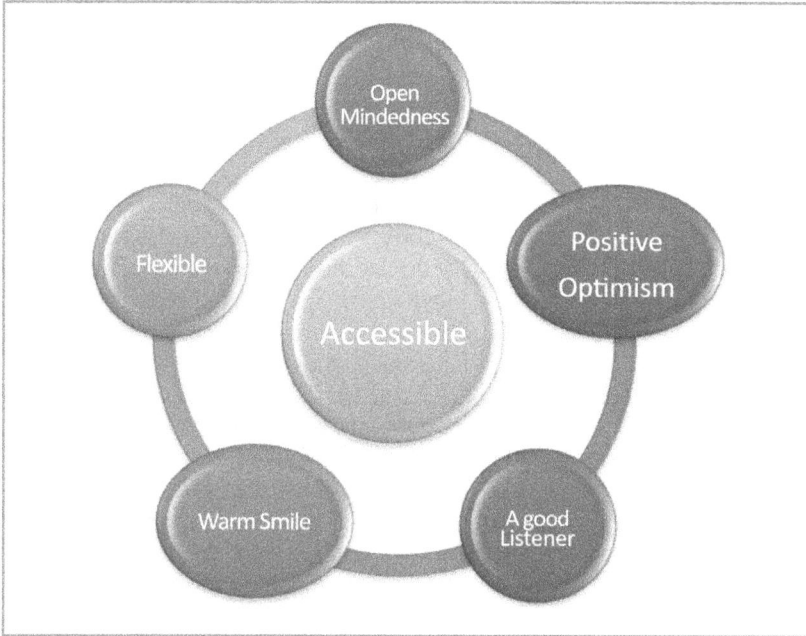

Book resource: *Lead Well and Prosper: 15 successful strategies for becoming a good boss. (2007). By Nick McCormick*

97

Confident

This is having the certainty that a course of action, a decision or an approach is the correct one given the circumstances.

Behavioural Indicators	Quick Tips For Skill Development
Has a positive self image	Cultivate a positive outlook to life. Although life does give its share of setbacks, there is a lot going for you. List up to 20 things you have done that you are proud of to affirm your ability to succeed and handle difficulty situations.
Is assertive and has a point of view	Confidently give your opinion or point of view on issues. Give a well balanced evaluation of the issue at hand whilst making it clear where you stand on an issue. Don't just be a "me-too" person as it gives the impression that you are lazy and not ready to think.
A self assured approach	Have an idea of the possible options available, the outcomes and impact of such outcomes. Carry out a risk analysis and put things in context by asking - what is the worst thing that could happen?
Is knowledgeable and competent in a certain field	Become a lifelong learner - always pursuing to improve yourself. Take self development seriously as it raises your personal competence levels which goes a long way in making you a reference point.
Is sought after for opinions on specific or general topics	Cultivate confidence in your own field of work and provide opinions through articles, talks or participating in discussions that help build your brand as a reference point. Network with others in your field and find out about relevant associations that you can join and make a contribution.

Skills that have a high positive impact on the ability to be *confident* include:

▶ **A good track record -** a repository of achievements in past roles or activities provides a basis for feeling confident to achieve future success. The confidence that comes from the knowledge that it is possible to achieve future results comes from the knowledge that you have done it before.

▶ **Competent -** high levels of competence allow one to exercise "knowledge power" and also provide a solid foundation to fall back to when faced with challenges or new problems.

▶ **Self-assured -** an individual who is self assured has that inner belief that things will work out and is sure of what they do. This self trust allows individuals to put themselves forward to tackle issues that somebody else lacking this skill would not attempt.

▶ **Assertive -** individuals that are assertive tend to be confident in themselves and do not shy away from stating their point of view. Assertive people are also likely to make suggestions and give ideas as well as challenge others.

▶ **Positive Affirmation -** affirmation is the ability to encourage oneself and have self talk that confirms that the action one is taking is the right one. Lack of positive affirmation leads to the inner critique taking over and replaying the possibility of failure which could lead to discouragement.

Supporting Behaviours for Confident

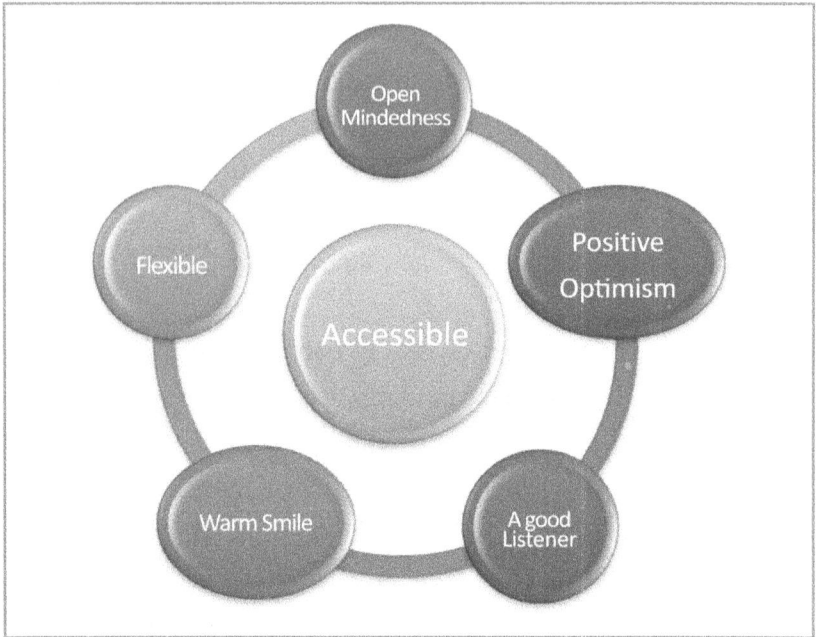

Book resource: *The Confidence Plan: How to build a stronger you (2005).*
By Tim Ursiny

Analytical

An objective, logical and systematic way of assessing multiple aspects of a proposal, problem or initiative.

Behavioural Indicators	Quick Tips For Skill Development
Incorporates multiple perspectives in assessing a situation or issue	Look for precedents, evidence of previous data on similar issues and put that together to build your case. Include perspectives that are outside your normal circle of options.
Reviews the pros and cons of any proposal to support decision making	Follow a structured approach - use rational methods of reviewing a situation. Learn to take the emotional aspects out of the analysis in the early stages and rely on data, then bring back the emotions at the end to help in decision making.
Utilizes analytical tools to surface trends and meaning in data	Learn to use a variety of analytical tools such as SWOT, PEST, Mind maps, Force Field analysis, Fish bone, asking why 5 times, etc. This brings additional objectivity in the decision making process.
Asks probing questions to understand root causes and not just symptoms	Become skillful at asking questions: asking who, when, where, what, how, why could lead to the unearthing of really meaningful information.
Has a great view of how separate parts fit together	Look for trends and correlation to other aspects. Identify cause and effect relationships. Highlight the insights coming out of this analysis and use this to arrive at objective conclusions.

Skills that have a high positive impact on the ability to be *analytical* include:

▶ **Use of Diagnostic tools** - the use of a variety of tools to review data and situations helps to bring out new perspectives that may not be obvious at first glance. Diagnostic tools help the decision making process by clarifying the pros and cons of various options.

▶ **Organized** - organized people tend to be more analytical. This is because analysis calls for logic and logic comes through systematic review of data or information. Organising data brings out trends and throws out insights that may not be clear when information is held in disparate formats.

▶ **Data Gathering** - analytical people also tend to be good at gathering the data they need to help in making sense out of a situation. Basic questions - Who, what, when, where, why and how can help gather adequate information to support decision making.

▶ **Creative** - improving your level of creativity strengthens your analysis. This is because creative people look at a set of data or information in unusual ways. They tend to ask "why not" and don't just stop at "why". Injecting creativity in the way work is done or decisions are arrived at improves the quality of analysis.

▶ **Integration** - the ability to integrate different aspects of seemingly unrelated information and trends tends to bring out new perspectives and hidden "wisdom" in ordinary data. The ability to integrate information is crucial for futuristic approaches and strategies and those that master this skill are able to predict the future more accurately.

Supporting Behaviours for Analytical

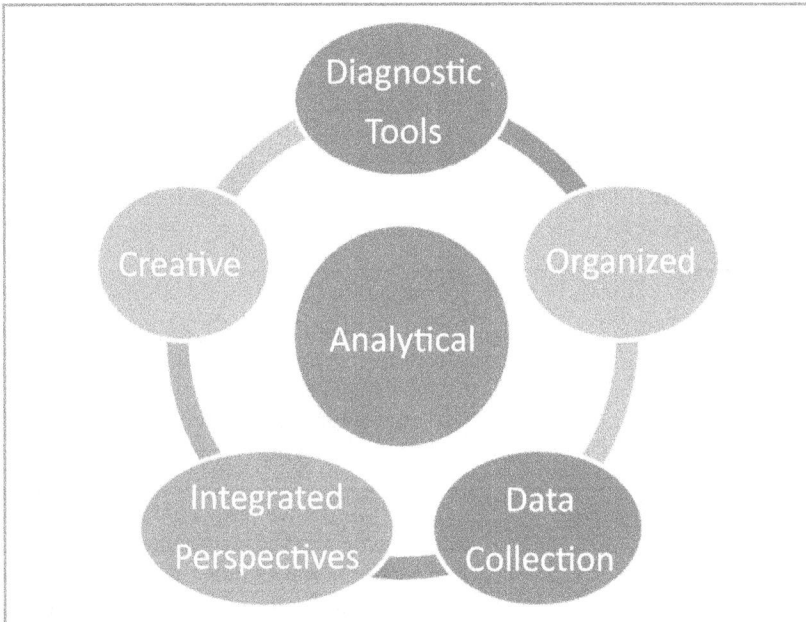

Book resource: *Developing Analytical Skills: Case studies in Management; by Dr B. Natarajan & S.K. Nagarajan (2007)*

Collaborative

Champions teamwork and the spirit of cooperation.

Behavioural Indicators	Quick Tips For Skill Development
Pushes for win/win solutions	Design projects that require collaboration and team work to be successful and make sure that no one team can do it by itself. One team member's failure will lead to total failure and the team has to work together in order to win.
Encourages teams to come together and solve problems rather than adopting a "lone ranger approach"	Consciously build team activities and projects to bring people together. Schedule team building activities in the course of work.
Elicits support from a broad range of stakeholders	Continually communicate who is doing what and the status of various projects to keep the team informed of what is happening. Lack of communication creates an environment for rumours which undermines collaboration.
Builds a climate of trust	Learn how to deal with conflict by developing conflict management skills instead of leaving conflict to arrive at its own resolution. Encourage celebrations for team wins.
Appreciates how individual actions impact different interest groups	Understand the goals and desires of different stakeholders. Define what success would look like for each stakeholder and look for opportunities to explore a "third option".

Skills that have a high positive impact on the ability to be *Collaborative* include:

▶ **Networking** - building relationships across different areas makes collaboration rather easy. Keep a record of key contacts that you have and make a habit of calling them or writing to them at least once every quarter just to stay in touch. When you genuinely need their help, it will be easier to get in touch with them and it will not feel like you are intruding.

▶ **Trust** - creating an environment of trust leads to great relationships and makes it easier to collaborate. Business takes place faster where there is trust. Without trust, agreements need to be typed, lawyers may need to be involved and numerous meetings are needed to arrive at a single point of agreement.

▶ **Communication** - communication is the bedrock of relationship building. Keeping stakeholders and other interest groups up to date on what is happening and providing them the information behind your arguments and decisions makes it easier to appreciate your stand point.

▶ **Diversity and Inclusion** - individuals filter information based on their previous experiences and their socialisation. An appreciation that different interest groups would view the same information with a slight difference is important in building collaboration.

▶ **A shared Vision** - it is essential to identify areas of common ground and specific instances where teams have a shared understanding. Even when there are differences of opinion on certain subjects and issues, the key is in capitalising on common goals and vision at every opportunity while acknowledging the differences and committing to work on areas of differences.

Supporting Behaviours for Collaborative

Book resource: *Collaboration handbook: creating, sustaining and enjoying the journey; by Michael Winer & Karen Kay (2003)*

Driven to Deliver

Ability to develop and deliver effective solutions in a timely manner to support and meet set objectives

Behavioural Indicators	Quick Tips For Skill Development
Follows through on promises	Learn to differentiate follow up from follow through. Follow up is just a confirmation as to what is happening and focuses on activities. Follow through focuses on the final goal and "busyness" does not equate to results. Those that follow through get results whilst those that follow up have information to back up any delays or excuses.
Sets clear goals	Setting Wildly Important Goals (WIGS) differentiates those that get results from those that don't. WIGS are goals that must be achieved no matter what and if they are not achieved nothing else matters. Normally they would be just 2 or 3 such goals but they make all the difference.
Maintains status updates in the form of scorecards, milestone updates to indicate current achievements	Results oriented people maintain status updates in all manner of forms - trackers, planners, to-do-lists, reminders, scorecards or milestones. Identify what works for you and make it a habit. It is said that a "short pencil is better than a long memory". Don't just rely on your memory, note it down and do it.
Proactive in dealing with new information	There is always new information coming in and those that adopt a perfectionist approach tend to never complete their work. Adopt the 80:20 rule and use the 20% information that is most important. Learn to ignore information that will have no significant impact on results in order to avoid analysis paralysis.

Anticipates blockages and comes up with alternative approaches for achieving results	Encountering a blockage in the pursuit of goals is normal. Learn to use problem solving techniques to identify possible obstacles - shortage of funds or other resources and always ask yourself what you would drop if you had less time, money or resources.
Understand what you are Accountable for and what you are responsible for	Accountability and responsibility are different. When you are the one expected to do the design, planning and delivery of a piece of work you are responsible. When you are managing teams that are doing the work you are accountable but your team members are responsible. This differentiation helps determine what you will do on a day to day basis. When this differentiation is not clear, managers do the work of their direct reports leaving the critical work of managing and leading undone whilst making team members feel micro-managed.

Skills that have a high positive impact on the ability to be **Driven to deliver** include:

▶ **Problem Solving -** the people that tend to achieve results are good in problem solving. They know who the "go to person" is when they encounter certain problems. They are familiar with what they can change and what they have to just take in to account in their plans and therefore don't spend time trying to influence change on areas that are non-negotiable.

▶ Understand the business - it is important to understand the business and what is a priority at any one time. If the organisation changes their scope from servicing mass markets and an individual spends most of the day coming up with strategies to target the wealth at the "bottom of the pyramid", this will be wasted time. Keep tabs and be in the know about what is happening in your organisation.

▶ **Sense of Urgency -** having a sense of urgency and injecting speed and pace in the way things are done is crucial in today's world where speed to market has become a mantra. It is better to deliver results ahead of time than to always scramble for last minute work which could be prone to errors and unforeseen obstacles.

▶ **Ask for help -** often times individuals feel as if asking for help is an admission that they can't do the job. Asking for help ensures that all the resources needed to get results are deployed and is a sign of a mature leader or manager—it is not about who but what. Ego is normally the problem that stands between managers and leaders when they don't ask for help as they want to get all the credit.

109

▶ **Chunking -** chunking refers to the skill of breaking down a goal in to smaller parts so as to ensure full focus on the most important next activity. When a goal is big and will take time to achieve, keeping an eye on only the end goal can be draining. Breaking the main goal in to sub-goals and celebrating wins as you achieve these sub goals maintains momentum and a drive for results.

Supporting Behaviours for Driven to deliver

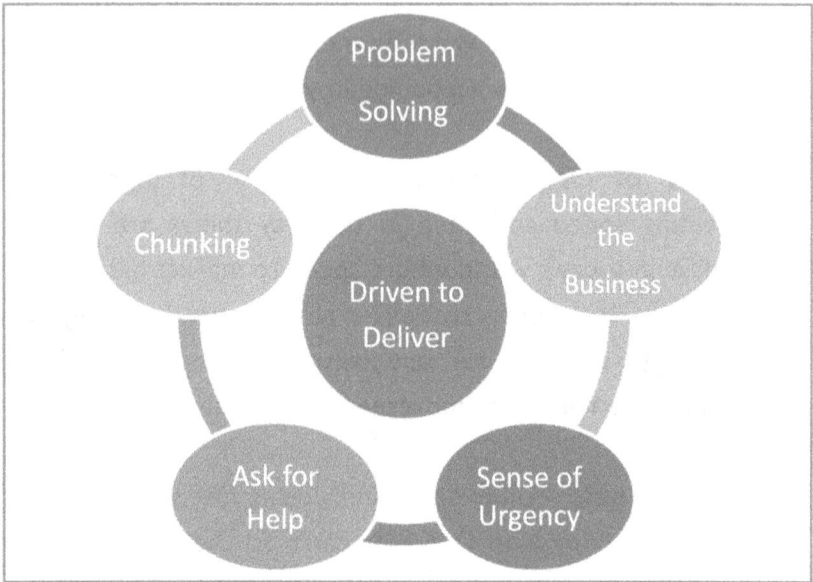

Book resource: Delivering Results: A new mandate for Human Resource professionals; by David Ulrich (1998)

Attention to Details

Ability to complete work using a systematic approach of testing the quality of work

Behavioural Indicators	Quick Tips For Skill Development
Maintains a system of checking for errors	Create your own system of checking your own work for errors. Some people complete a piece of work, leave it for a while or overnight and revisit it. This provides a fresh perspective and helps pinpoint mistakes. Another option is to print out work and read it as a hard copy and not just soft copy on screen - it is sometimes easier to spot gaps, errors and logic flow in this way.
Asks other people to help check the quality of work and provide input	Having a buddy or a team member check your work before you submit it increases the chances of accuracy. After working with the same set of information for a while, obvious errors can go unnoticed but a fresh set of eyes is likely to spot those errors.
Creates templates that help reduce the incidence of errors	Templates introduce a standardized way of presenting information and work. Such templates ensure all the key areas are covered in a report and aids completeness of work.
Starts with the end in mind	Be clear what a good piece of work looks like. Have quality thresholds that each piece of work has to pass before it is submitted. These could include double or even triple checks on the source of data and the accuracy of that data or similar checks.
Uses a checklist or set standards to authenticate work	Checklists ensure completeness of work and an effective way of ensuring all angles are covered. Checklists that indicate necessary sign offs, or specific steps that need to be taken help to speed up work whilst ensuring completeness of work. This contributes to an individual's attention to details.

Skills that have a high positive impact on the ability to demonstrate *Attention to Details* include:

▶ **Create "Gates"** - having work go through a number of gates helps ensure completeness, accuracy and consistency with the bigger picture. Project teams normally create such gates to provide a number of levels where information and quality of work is checked with a different perspective and by the end of the process, the work would have gone through a great deal of thorough checks.

▶ **Dry runs** - the habit of carrying out dry-runs either of presentations or meetings helps point out gaps in data or information or logic flaws that can be addressed prior to the actual session. Preparedness created in this way helps to cover all the key areas.

▶ **Anticipate Questions** - creating FAQs and coming up with the possible answers helps to ensure all the important aspects of a situation are covered. Anticipating questions leads to searching for additional data and information to support responses. FAQs also force individuals to present information with the end user in mind and therefore ensure a better level of preparedness.

▶ **Logic Flow** - asking three basic questions will ensure that work presented is logical and is structured in a way to speed up decision making. These questions are; What? So What? What next? The first question, what, helps to set context of the data, information or report; the second question, so what, is driven at sense making and confirms why this information or data is important; and, what next, provides an opportunity to make a recommendation, ask for resources or request for approval.

▶ **Packaging -** the way work is presented is very important. It elicits confidence in the eyes of the receiver that a lot of effort has gone in to the work. The structure of a report, the way a PowerPoint presentation is organized, the font and the way it feels to read the work all go towards determining the level of credibility attached to the work. Any spelling errors, wrong dates, or titles have to be removed. The report or presentation always has to tell a story. Ask yourself, what story am I presenting?

Supporting Behaviours for Attention to Details

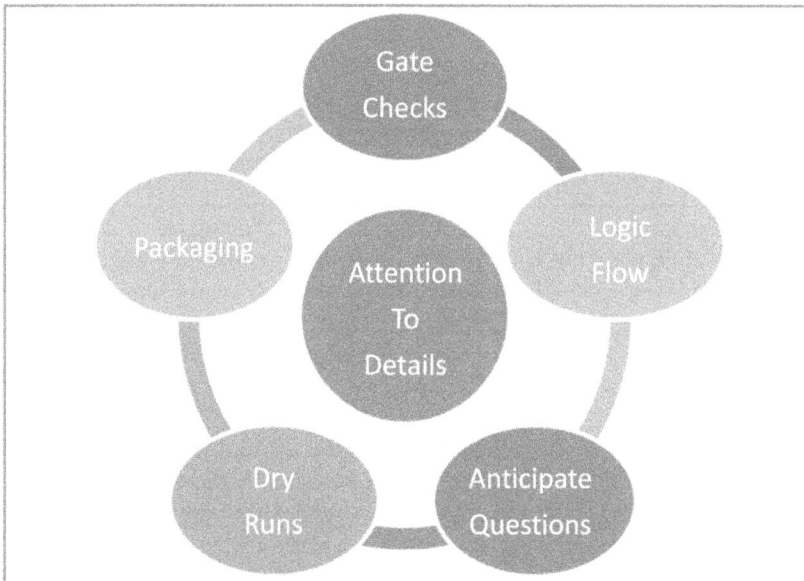

Book resource: *The Little Big Things: 163 ways to Pursue Excellence; by Tom Peters (2010)*

Flexible

Ability to expand options and possible solutions within an existing decision making frameworks.

Behavioural Indicators	Quick Tips For Skill Development
Open to receive new information and evidence	Develop an open mindset. Open mindedness is not the same as indecisiveness. Be accessible and adopt a listening stand to attract new information. Such information is critical especially during times of change.
Willingness to change especially when it is clear that existing processes and policies are not appropriate	Be open even to unconventional ways of doing things. Just because you have not done it before or nobody else has ever done it is not reason enough to block it out. Be open to try new ways of doing thing.
Able to deal with difficult people and situations	Validate dissenting views. Try and find out why people have a different perspective from the one you hold. Carry out research and get additional data to understand where the other party's arguments are coming from. Acknowledging their concerns will help ensure that you are seen as flexible.
Generates various possible option and not just one or two options	Life is not an "either" "or" game. Third, fourth or even fifth options can lead to optimal decisions that result in the selection of the best result. At the same time, such solutions are likely to lead to win/win outcomes.
Walk in the shoes of the other party	Learn to step out of your comfort zone. Getting first hand information on a situation is extremely useful even if the final decision does not change as a result of this action. A better understanding of the situation always gives a feeling of empathy and care towards the party involved.

Skills that have a high positive impact on the ability to be *flexible* include:

▶ **Customer Orientated** - having the final customer or stakeholders at heart when performing tasks or arriving at decisions ensures that it is not just a case of "us" and "them" but rather a case of what is best for all of us.

▶ **Integrity** - integrity is the compass that ensures that regardless of the level of flexibility exhibited ethics and values are at the centre of decisions. Even in cases where individuals are inflexible, as long as they maintain a high level of integrity, the dissenting party is likely to accept the outcome. The desire for flexibility should not violate integrity principles and individuals should not pursue flexibility for the sake of it.

▶ **Relationships** - building and creating strong relationships provides an inbuilt system of flexibility that does not necessarily need to be negotiated. Individual tend to be more flexible when dealing with those they have strong relationships with. Building strong relationships will therefore aid the ability to be perceived as flexible.

▶ **Analytical** - developing the capability to view situations in an analytical way increases the possibility of being flexible. This is because analytics provide data on options and outcomes and having analysed what the impact of certain decisions will be, it is easier to adopt a give and take stand and be willing to forgo certain items without necessarily losing out.

▶ **Long term perspective** - maintaining a long term perspective ensures that what look like short term setbacks can be accommodated as long as they don't adversely affect the long term goal. In the short term, some flexibility could be build in project delivery which may result in losing ground in the short term but may actually develop the necessary allies for achieving longer term goals. If the analysis is such that conceding on the one or two issues will make it easier to gain ground in future, then maintaining a long term perspective would support adopting a flexible approach.

Supporting Behaviours for Flexible

Book resource: *AdaptAbility: How to Survive change you didn't ask for by M.J. Ryan (2009)*

Visionary

Ability to paint a picture of the future and influence/rally people to desire and create that future

Behavioural Indicators	Quick Tips For Skill Development
Asks what if questions	Visionary people are dreamers and likely to adopt blue sky thinking. They are not limited to the way things are today and are ready to embrace options that will create a desired future. Learn to test hypothesis and embrace possibilities by asking 'what if' questions. Step back every once in a while and take some time to reflect.
Ability to spot cross cutting issues and trends	Learn to spot trends both internally and externally in order to use these to shape or redefine the vision. It is easier to paint a picture of the future if there is integration of information from various sources rather than adopting a narrow perspective.
Influences people to desire a future state	Effectively paint a picture of the future and link it to what individuals' desire. If individuals can see how the achievement of the vision will affect them positively they are more likely to follow. Measure how far you are from achieving the vision and communicate this to maintain enthusiasm.
Effectively communicates what the future will be like	Share the vision in a prolific manner to everyone and not just a few people. Ensure the vision can be stated in a short statement or summarized in a few words such that every individual can connect to that vision.
Adopts a helicopter view or birds eye	Maintain the bigger picture. Every action has consequences and impact that may not necessarily be quantifiable. Don't get stuck in the detail, step back and look at the total picture and inter relationships between people, data or processes.

117

Skills that have a high positive impact on the ability to be **Visionary** include:

▶ **Learning -** become a life-long learner. Remain abreast with what is happening inside and outside the business or function. Spot trends that may affect the future and help shape individual or the organisation's vision. The attitude of learning increases the level of knowledge which is essential in shaping visions.

▶ **Futuristic -** visions are about the future. An obsession with the past can paralyse future action. Look back to learn but focus on the future. Make the pictures of the future as vivid as possible and communicate them with people. A picture of a great future can be really energising especially during the early days when results are not necessarily obvious.

▶ **Reflect -** standing back from the main action and reviewing what is happening and whether activities are in line with the vision is a great activity to undertake. Most often leaders don't find the time to reflect because situations tend to unravel rather fast and due to the speed of change and need to make decisions by the hour or even minute, reflection time can be a real luxury. However, time spend reflecting is critical in ensuring the vision does not just remain a dream but it becomes a reality.

▶ **Belief -** a strong sense of belief in ones goals ensures confidence in communicating a vision. Without belief there would be no conviction to share and influence others to rally behind the vision. A high level of belief increases the dependability index of an individual and the ability to be trusted. Developing belief in your goals will determine whether or not you get followers behind your vision.

▶ **Communication** - the ability to influence, excite and bring life to the vision will determine how successful one is in marshalling the necessary support for the vision. The power to tell stories and identify analogies that are effective in painting a clear picture will make it easy for followers to identify with the vision.

Supporting Behaviours for Visionary

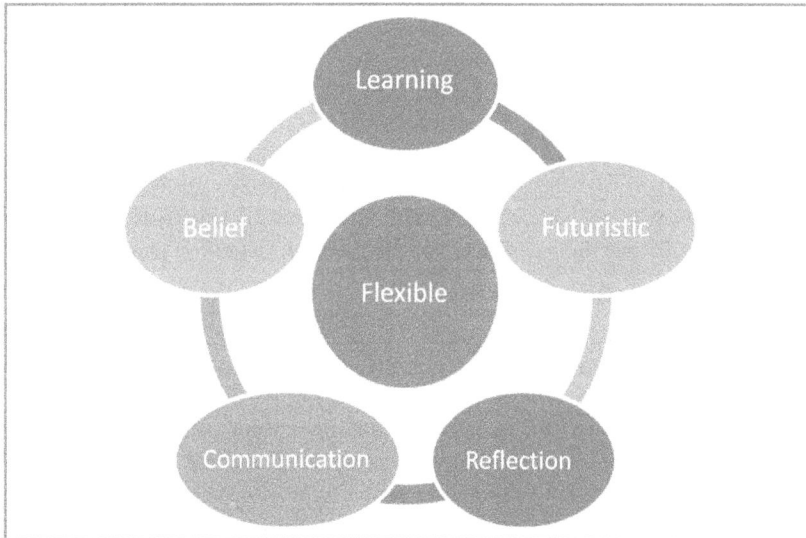

Book resource: *Visionary Leadership: Getting a Compelling sense of direction for your organisation; By Burt Nanus (1992)*

Curious

Ability to remain inquisitive and ask questions that challenge the status quo

Behavioural Indicators	Quick Tips For Skill Development
Keeps abreast with what is happening around them	Talk to people; find out what is happening in their parts of the business. Ask them for opinions about activities that are taking place inside and outside the business. Remain open to new ideas that you gather in your interactions and use these to shape your work or perspective.
Maintains a stock of knowledge on trends and opportunities	Keep a record of interesting data or statistics and information that you gather in various places. When something catches your eye endeavour to find out more about it. These activities help you to remain curious and therefore up to date with what is happening.
Asks "what if" to unearth possibilities	Learn to ask questions and then listen for opportunities to add value. A deeper level of listening will enable you to get more information than the superficial day to day listening that we do. Listen for pain, desires and dreams. What you hear can lead to dramatic changes in approach or focus.
Challenges the status quo	The fact that things have always been done in a certain way is not necessarily bad but changes are always taking place which means that processes, systems and procedures ought to keep up to date with such changes. Proactively schedule sessions to question why things are done in a certain way within your function or business.
Remains open to new ideas and remains flexible	Read innovation magazines or news on discoveries taking place in your area of work. Spot ideas that may be applicable in your field. Learn to borrow ideas from other organisations or other parts of your business and tailor them to your own work.

Skills that have a high positive impact on the ability to be **Curious** include:

▶ **Innovation** - creative people and those that are open to innovations tend to be more curious. Any innovation or discovery calls for remaining open to new ideas and ways of doing things. Innovation comes with change and those that thrive during times of change are the curious ones.

▶ **Ask Questions** - asking questions is probably the most visible and the easiest way of remaining curious. Apart from the "who, where, how, when" questions; the question, why, often surfaces deep seated beliefs, values and convictions that can explain the reasons behind an action or decision. Beliefs and values are often stumbling blocks in driving successful change processes and gaining this information is critical to support the design of initiatives to deal with resistance to change.

▶ **Open Mindset** - remaining open to new ideas and ways of doing things will help develop your ability to remain curious. When you block opinions that are different from the ones that you hold, you effectively rule out the possibility of learning new and probably better ways of doing things.

▶ **Information gathering** - the habit of collecting information helps to ensure individuals remain up to date and relevant. In a world where change is taking place very fast and by the time a product gets to market, an organisation is supposed to already be working on an improved version of the product. The ability to remain relevant cannot therefore be over stated. Gathering information on trends in the market place will help keep an individual or a business ahead of the game.

▶ **Networking** - maintaining a network of contacts in various aspects ensures that you stay on the trajectory of change. Such networks act as a source information and that information remains fresh and relevant.

Supporting Behaviours for Curiosity

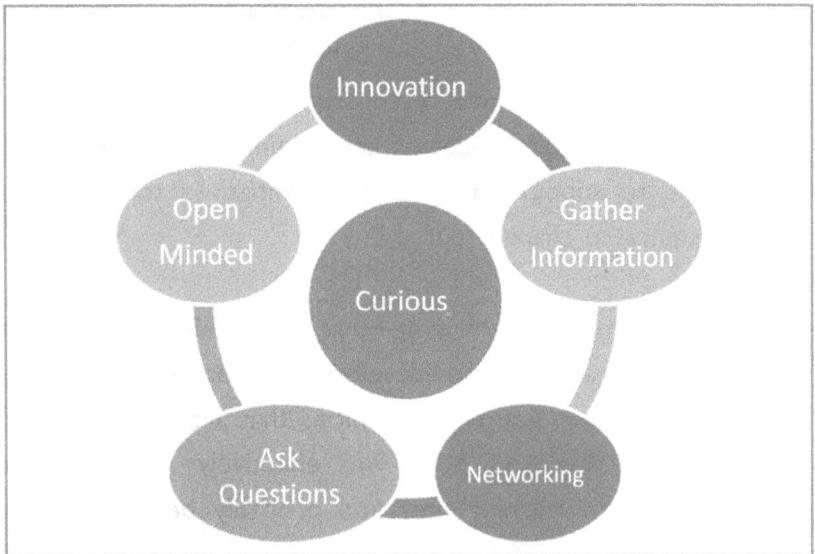

Book resource: *Curious? Discover the missing ingredient to a fulfilling life by Todd Kash Dan (2009)*

Caring

Ability to value people and the contribution they bring thereby sharing information and working to ensure that decisions taken minimize negative impact on people.

Behavioural Indicators	Quick Tips For Skill Development
Empathizes with people	Improve your level of Emotional Quotient (EQ) to allow you to hear more than what is actually said. Check for meaning beyond words and get to the real fears that people have and communicate to address those fears. Acknowledge both what is said and what is not said as both are just as important.
Brings the people perspective to bear when making decisions	Always appreciate the impact decisions will have on people both on the short term as well as the long run. This does not mean that because decisions have a negative impact on people they will not be taken, but rather having this perspective helps in the selection of options in the decision making processes.
Treats people with dignity	Respect for people is probably the most important factor that gives evidence that one cares. People want to be treated as human beings and not just employee numbers or head count. Treating people with dignity even when they make mistakes gives an indication to all others that you care for people just because they are people.
Is approachable and open to feedback	Learn to suspend judgment when listening to an individual. Don't listen with an intention to answer but rather with the intention to hear and learn. Remain open to receiving feedback by creating the opportunity to get this feedback even when the feedback is negative.
Sharing relevant information	Provide information and let people know what is happening and how it affects them. When people know both what is happening but also why it is being done, they are more likely to buy in to the process and support it.

123

Skills that have a high positive impact on the ability to be **Caring** include:

▶ **Accessible** - accessible people are said to be more caring. It is difficult to convey a sense that you care from a remote distance. When people have access to their leaders and can approach them when they have any issue, there is a real sense that they are cared for. This sense of accessibility is the one that creates a "family setting" in businesses, a sense that we are in this together.

▶ **Listening** - the opportunity to give feedback and contribute ideas makes us feel heard. At times those contributions may not even be implemented but the fact that someone took the time to listen to us makes us feel appreciated and important. Listening to people gives them a sense that you care for them.

▶ **Supportive** - knowing that someone has your back and your best interests at heart is at the core of the feeling of being cared for. The reason why family bonds are so strong is because with family, we know they will do that which is right for us. That sense of support that we know we can count on gives a real sense that someone cares.

▶ **Integrity** - a high level of integrity increases the level of general trust amongst individuals or teams. Knowing that the people we deal with will act with integrity assures us that they will not act in ways that will give them an advantage at our expense. Integrity therefore raises the sense that people care about us.

▶ **Communication** - without communication, it is difficult to confirm if one cares for you or not. The things we say, the way we say it, time we select to convey the information all give indications of how much we care about the individuals in scope. Remain deliberate in how you demonstrate that you care and set aside opportunities to appreciate teams or individuals that have made a contribution that you value.

Supporting Behaviours for Caring

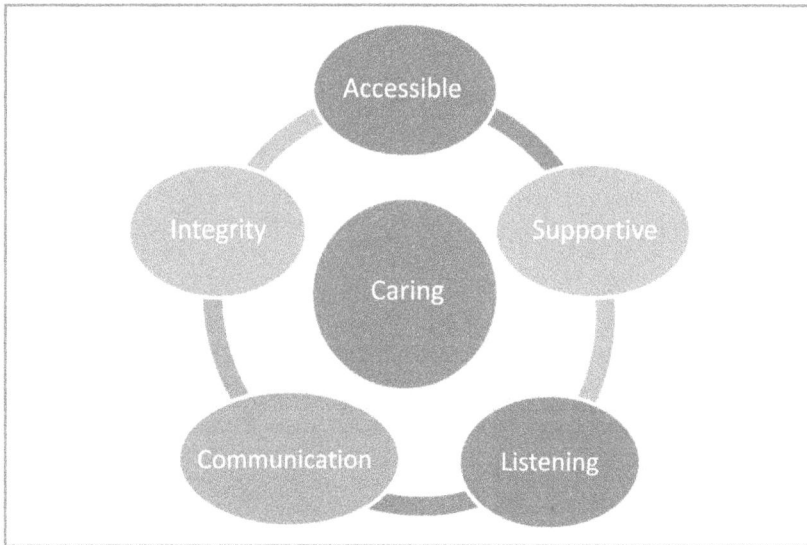

Book resource: *Caring enough to hear and be heard; How to hear and how to be heard in equal communication by David Augsburger (2009)*

125

Part Five

A Seat At The Table

The current dynamics in the business arena coupled with constant change in the organisational landscape calls for the HR professional to support the organisation to successfully navigate through constant change. From the research findings, there are great expectations placed on the HR function by HR's key stakeholders; CEOs and Line Managers. This expectation has influenced the kind of skills that are now considered critical for HR professionals.

From the study, it is clear that the priority skills for success in the Human Resource practice are **effective communicator, personal credibility and relationship builder**. These three skills could be said to be the "legs of the stool" on which the HR professional sits at the strategy table. As Meisinger (2003) states, "other competencies may get one a top job in HR but credibility will keep one there". Technical competencies are important and are the reason that HR gets invited to the table in the first instance; however, it is the effective use of behavioural skills that will guarantee the success of the HR professional and have the greatest impact in the organisation.

129

The HR professional has a wide range of stakeholders and the overall success is determined by the ability to influence them. To name a few of the stakeholders:

▶ The CEO
▶ The Board
▶ The management team
▶ Line Managers

- ▶ Labour Unions
- ▶ Recruitment Agencies
- ▶ Training institutions
- ▶ Colleges and Universities that provide graduates
- ▶ Government agencies and Ministries

The credible activist competency identified by Ulrich (2008) is said to be the top predictor for outstanding performance of an HR professional. This competency is actually a combination of the following behavioural skills: *effective communicator, relationship builder, personally credible, confident and courage to challenge*. Ulrich states that the credible activist competence is the "deal breaker" and without it nothing else matters. This makes being a credible activist a wildly important objective for any HR professional who is keen to have fast, positive and significant impact.

The Credible Activist Skill Unpacked

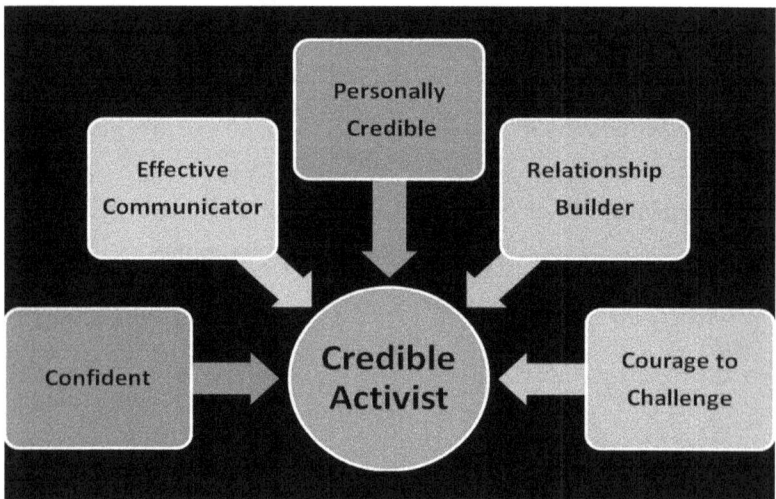

As Ulrich, et al., (2010) intimate, the priorities of CEOs include **talent management, leadership, strategy execution, managing change and organisational capability.** HR professionals hold the key to unlocking all the above mentioned activities in the organisation. Of the five priorities presented, only two call for technical competences *(talent management and building organisational capability)* whereas the remaining three call for the strategic use of soft skills. Successful **leadership** has at its core some of the behavoural skills such as **visionary, influencing, communicating, building trust** and being **credible.** To effectively **manage change**, the ability to **build relationships, communicate** and **influence** is critical to gain buy-in and momentum towards successful management change. **Strategy execution** is about **translating strategy** in to day to day activities and effectively cascading this throughout the organisation.

Grossman (2007) rightly states that "Legacy HR work is going, and HR people who don't change with it will be gone". There is an urgent need for HR professionals to up skill and keep up with the changing expectations of the profession. The transition taking place in the HR profession comes with a shift of emphasis in terms of the skill set needed to succeed in today's workplace. Unfortunately, many of the institutions of learning that train HR professionals are still focused only on the technical competencies and do not dedicate time to behavioural skills. What would really contribute to HR up skilling is for future HR professionals to go through training and assessment on their soft skills capabilities as part of the accreditation process in to the profession.

The three core skills identified earlier *(effective communicator, personally credible and relationship builder)* ought to be an integral part of any recruitment, selection, development and promotion process for HR practitioners. These skills are the support system that gives the HR professional a voice at the strategy table.

HR at the Strategy Table

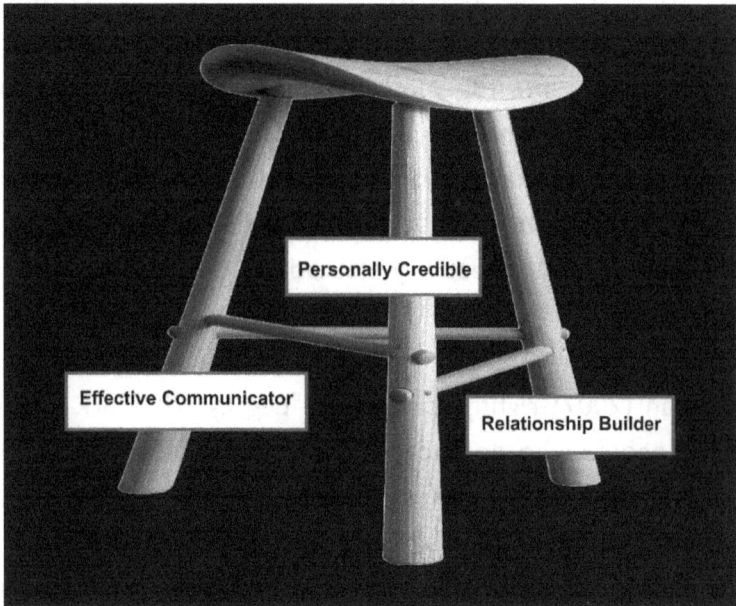

Vickers (2007) confirms that for HR professionals to be successful, they need to get in the game and engage in conversations about what the business needs to do to grow and succeed. Such conversations are only possible when the HR professional is credible, effective in communication and has build relationships that allow for them to be invited to the conversation table in the first instance.

Organisations are run through crucial conversations that take place at various forums and the art of influencing during these conversations is what will differentiate one HR professional from the next. For HR to positively impact the business the function needs clout and it is soft skills that open the door for accessing and utilizing this clout. As Sparrow & Marchington (1998) state, "only when they have earned and rebuilt trust, will HR practitioners be in a stronger position to exert their authority and contribute to what are decisive times within organisations". Unfortunately, the research results indicate that at this point in time, HR skill development is not yet refined enough or effectively targeted to address the needs of practitioners. Respondents from most of the countries surveyed primarily use on-the-job skill development. This approach tends to be rather unstructured and does not guarantee effective skill development.

Effective Behavioural Skills Development for HR Professionals

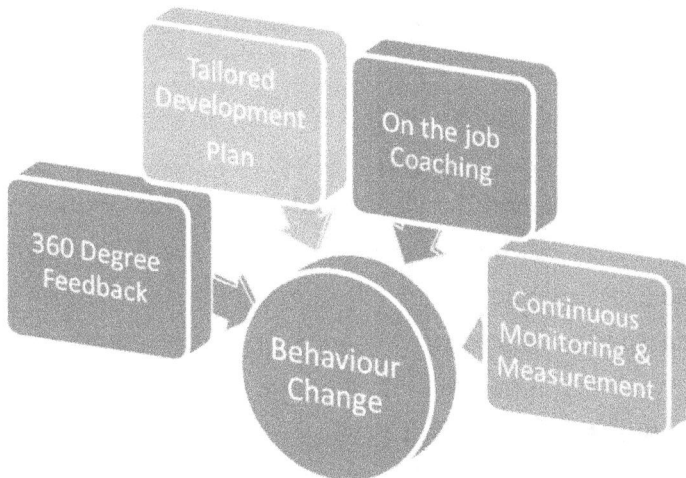

A more structured approach to behavioural skill development would involve the use of **"deliberate practice"** where 360 degree feedback processes are employed to determine current skill levels. The gaps identified are then followed by tailored individual development plans and on-the-job coaching. Continued monitoring and measurement would provide an effective avenue and path for up skilling HR professionals on these skills.

For HR practitioners, 360 degree feedback would come from a variety of sources. Apart from assessments from the traditional stakeholders—self, line manager, peers and direct reports; additional feedback from a few of the employees or union representatives could provide additional perspectives normally left out in 360 degree feedback. For the senior executive in HR, feedback on how HR is perceived in the business on various aspects can provide the information needed to move up the ladder on strategic partnering. For instance, feedback on whether the Human Resource function is visible, whether it has impact or it is trusted to do what is right for the employee can provide real useful information for transforming the function.

Based on the results from the 360 degree feedback, an individualised and tailored development plan can be drawn up for each HR practitioner. The plan would include areas of behavioural strengths that can be exploited to benefit the business and any soft skills that would need further improvement. The plan would include specific experiences, exposure or training programmes that the practitioner would need to participate in order to realise the set development goals.

As part of the development plan, the use of on-the-job coaching by either the Line Manager or an external coach would further support this structured skill development. Coaching ensures that the specific behaviours that need to be improved are prioritised and opportunities to try out the new skill are proactively identified. Like any other development plan, what gets measured gets done and incorporating an ongoing monitoring and measurement system to track behaviour change would help catalyze learning.

The use of this integrated approach to behavioural skill development is recommended because of the multifaceted approach it introduces in the process. As already discussed, survey data confirms that *feedback* and *coaching* are the most effective methods of changing behaviour. Behavioural competencies (soft skills) are the missing ingredient that will empower the HR professional to spark passion and raise the energy levels in the organisation. Energy creates motion and without motion there is no passion. Effective HR practitioners have to play the role of "energy managers"–managing the energy level in the organisation. When you walk through the corridors of a business or attend a meeting even in a place that is totally unfamiliar to you, it is not difficult to sense the kind of energy in the environment.

135

Employee engagement is all about managing energy and passion. When there is a lot of negative energy in a business, it distracts people from focusing on the priorities and goals of the business. The HR professional, acting as the 'energy manager', would come up with strategies to cool the temperature in an organisation that is characterised by negative energy e.g. boycotts, stage ins, picketing, etc. In some instances though the opposite problem occurs where there is just no energy in an organisation and apathy rules. The 'energy manager' would work towards raising the energy levels of employees by tapping in to their passions and effectively drive up productivity and engagement in the business. It is the effective management of the energy in a business that leads to winning the hearts and minds of employees and turning them in to raving fans of the organisation they work in—true ambassadors of the brand, products and vision of the business. The three stakeholders; CEO, HR professionals and Line Managers all have a part to play in managing this energy but HR has a core role due to the unique position as the organisation's culture custodian.

Part Six

THE FUTURE OF HUMAN RESOURCE PRACTICE

The HR landscape has changed. The evolution that has been taking place within the profession over the last twenty years or so has got to a place where the day-by-day role of the HR professional has changed. The problem is that a few years ago, many Personnel Departments simply rebranded themselves as Human Resource departments without necessarily transforming or repositioning themselves in the business. The inconsistency and low standards in HR practice that is delivered by such practitioners has led to many questioning the credibility of HR and has placed the profession in a position where it has to prove its worth. The outcome has been a reduction in the ability of the HR practitioners' to contribute to and influence strategy creation and execution.

Positioning and Expectations

In today's world of work, the positioning of the HR function and the corresponding expectations of the function have also changed. HR practitioners now have a *seat at the table*. The value HR brings to the table should therefore be visible to all with the kind of impact that is clear for all to see. However, there is still a view today that HR is a cost centre and the value it creates is not as significant as the contribution to the employee cost line. Previously, the profession was more administrative and the expectation was that all HR would do is just deliver on the basics; make sure people are paid accurately and on time, process and maintain leave and holiday records, administer medical benefits and enforce disciplinary and grievance procedures. In summary, the view of HR practitioners was that they were merely policy administrators in the business.

The current and old positioning of HR is giving way to a future where instead of having Human Resource or Human capital departments, we would see more of Culture departments and People management departments. This transition is driven by a need to bring back the "human" aspect in to people management and treat employees as people and not just resources. The concern here is that when the profession is referred to as Human Resource, there is an expectation that the professionals that manage the function have to exploit and extract value in the shortest possible time and at the lowest cost.

The transition to people management brings back the "human face" and provides an opportunity to restore dignity and respect in the way businesses treat the people that create organisational value. In line with this new positioning, in future the People Management function would be held accountable for bottom line results. The department provides guidance during the hiring process, has massive input in the talent development process, determines the reward that is paid to people and drives performance management. If all these processes are carried out well, the business is highly likely to succeed. With the function having so much influence on business performance, why isn't held accountable for business results? It is just a matter of time before the accountability for business results is as much the responsibility of HR as it is for the customer facing functions.

A Marketing Approach - the future of Human Resource Practice

The ongoing transformation in Human Resource practice seems to mirror the Marketing discipline. In Marketing, the customer is king; the focus is on developing products and services that not only meet customer needs but anticipate and exceed expectations. Communication is meant to emotionally connect with the customer and the capillarity of distribution channels ensures that the customer can access products almost anywhere and at any time.

Central in the minds of Human Resource professionals is the need to engage employees and get them to go above the contractual obligations as translated on their contract. Within the profession, the question is how well the concept of the internal customer has taken root. This would mean that HR policies, procedures and practices have to be tailored to meet employee needs. This marks a shift in the mindset of Human Resource practitioners to begin positioning policy and practice requirements from the eye of the employee and not just from the perspective of the business. This shift will require an artistic balance that ensures HR policy and practice meets the needs of both the business and the more demanding employee of the 21st century.

141

Once employees take the position of customers in the eyes of HR practitioners, HR initiatives need to be positioned like products and services that are subject to employee choice. Customers normally patronise those products that meet their needs and in the future, employees will demand the same—variety and choice of the offering made by HR. HR practitioners would then re-examine how they design the products and services they offer to employees. A lot more research will need to be undertaken to ensure that HR products and services are developed based on adequate insight from employees. Focus group discussions and feedback sessions will be necessary to ensure employee views are encapsulated in the final product. Although a lot of consultation is taking place today before HR introduces new products and services, the process is expected to evolve even faster and place the employee at the core of product design.

When HR initiatives are viewed as products, it becomes easy to package and brand them for employees to understand the specific attributes of each product or service and the benefits encapsulated in each offering. Practically all the initiatives that come from HR can be viewed this way thereby lending themselves to the application of marketing tactics to ensure they meet and exceed employee expectations. Every single HR initiative can be viewed as a product and service: the introduction of a *recognition scheme, a savings scheme, a coaching program, a newsletter, an incentive scheme or a cascade of company values*.

142

The push to automate HR services and introduce e-HR options ensures employees can access the information they need from remote locations. Virtual HR is becoming a reality and remote access to HR systems offers the kind of flexibility that is aligned to the employee of the 21st century. Employees can select and schedule their own online training, update their personal data online, apply for jobs that come up and schedule their holidays using automated systems. In the same vein as banking customers that use internet banking to check their balances and make fund transfer online or mobile phone customers who can use "mobile money" and pay for transactions from their phones, employees are demanding for the same level of convenience and access to the systems used in the workplace.

With the increased use of virtual working teams, flexi working arrangements and working from home; the need for employees to use online systems will substantially increase in the future. HR functions that don't prepare well for this will find it increasingly difficult to attract and retain certain types of talent and may compromise their competitive edge.

Promoting products and services and providing adequate publicity is at the core of Marketing functions as they understand the impact this has on product and service uptake. If a customer does not know that a product or service exists, they won't purchase it. In order to influence consumer behaviour, Marketers have become very creative in the way they promote and present their products. The Human Resource function is being called upon to adopt a similar approach and market the products and services of HR to employees. It is not uncommon for employees to complain that the quality and quantity of communication in their organisation could be improved. Human Resource 'marketing' would ensure that a communication plan is put in place every time a new product or service is introduced or even at specific intervals to remind employees of the products and services on offer.

143

The Employee Centric Organisation

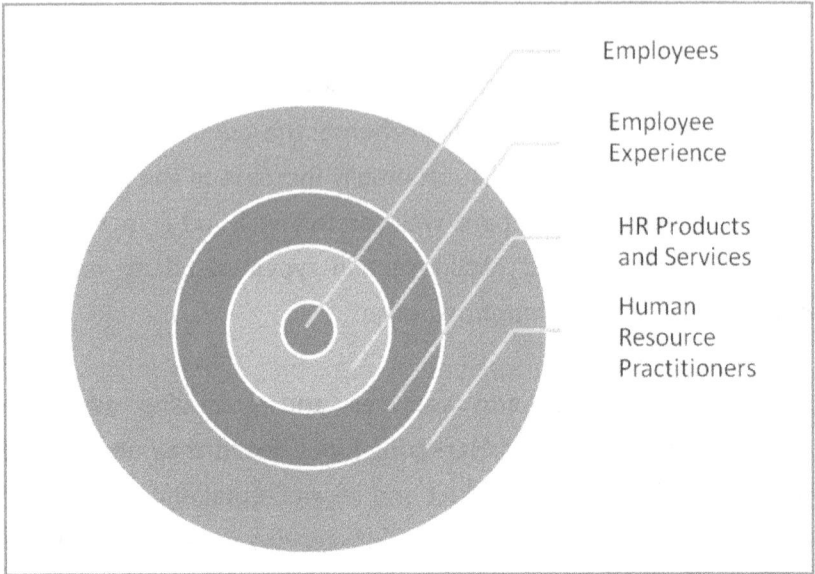

Employees

Employee
Experience

HR Products
and Services

Human
Resource
Practitioners

At the centre of Human Resource practice is the employee. Most organisations will declare that employees are the most important resource or asset they have but how many truly put the employees at the centre of their operations? With the increasing desire to meet the external customer demands, it has become rather obvious that the ways external customers experience an organisation is on the basis of how the employees in that organisation interact with them. Good customer service is often a reflection of the employee experience.

Research indicates that engaged employees deliver higher levels of customer experience and satisfaction as compared to apathetic or disengaged employees. With the increasing use of the balanced score card to measure the performance of executive teams, the customer satisfaction index and employee engagement score are gaining high visibility with share holders. In order to improve employee experience, HR can implement specific initiatives at every employee touch point (the points where employee emotionally connect with the employee) in the business. As an example, the employee entry point as experienced through the entire recruitment process, the induction as well as on boarding process are key touch points for an employee. Ensuring a good experience during this process is the first step in cultivating a culture of employee engagement.

Many other touch points such as the pay process, training and development experiences, performance management or even celebrating individual or team wins all create positive or negative employee experience. Targeted focus should be placed on ensuring employees get a positive feel of the workplace. Whether it is receiving a birthday card, a welcome cake after a long absence from work or a congratulatory letter from the line manager on exceeding a target; all these actions create a feeling of a "great place" to work in.

HR can put in place systems that make it easy to connect with employees and cultivate employee engagement, loyalty and retention. Such systems could include the design and development of HR products and services that meet or exceed employee expectations. The products and services that HR delivers should be easily understandable to employees. The HR professional that will succeed in an employee centric organisation will have the necessary technical skills to translate company strategy in to HR practice leading to the design of products and services that are aligned with the organisational priorities. At the same time, the HR professional will know how to package and communicate these products and services in a

145

way that will influence employees to patronize them. In this era of e-HR, the function can utilise technology to communicate and deliver a big portion of HR services through self service online systems. An HR professional with great soft skills will influence employees and create a culture that is receptive to the products and services that HR delivers.

In the same way that we have seen the introduction of HR System specialist roles, in the future there is a likelihood that we will witness the introduction of HR 'marketing' roles to help support the function in positioning itself to meet the needs of employees and place them at the centre of Human Resource practice. In the same way that customer experience is a measure of success when products and services are evaluated, employee experience will become a key measure to gauge the effectiveness of Human Resource functions.

Human Resource practitioners that will succeed are those that keep up with the changing HR landscape and remain ahead of the evolution curve by up skilling on soft skills and adopting employee centric approaches to Human Resource practice. The soft skills of the HR professionals will make or break the impact of the HR function. Soft skills are truly the deal breaker!

APPENDIX

RESEARCH QUESTIONNAIRE

1. Please select the type of respondent you represent.
    - ▶ CEO/General Manager
    - ▶ Line Manager
    - ▶ HR Professional

2. In which Country are you currently working?

    ....

HR BEHAVIOURAL SKILLS

3. The list of HR Behavioural skills presented below has been compiled from research by leading HR Executive Education Institutions. Select the top 7 skills you consider critical for the success of an HR professional. A successful HR professional should be:

Answer Options	Response
Accessible	
Analytical	
Attentive to Details	
Caring	
Collaborative / Inclusive	
An Effective Communicator	
Confident	
Courageous to Challenge	
Customer Orientated	
Curious	
Visionary	
Decisive	
Driven to Deliver	
Flexible/Adaptable	
Personally Credible	
A Relationship builder	
A Skilled Influencer	

4.   Insert any additional Behavioural Skills you consider critical for HR professionals that are not listed above.

CURRENT SKILL LEVEL OF HR PROFESSIONALS

5.   With reference to your current organisation, how would you score the general skill level of the staff in the HR department in regard to the skills listed below?

	Below Expectations	Average	Above Average	Excellent
Accessible				
Analytical				
Attention to Details				
Caring				
Collaborative / Inclusive				
Effective Communicator				
Confident				
Courage to Challenge				
Customer Orientated				
Curious				
Decisive				
Driven to Deliver				
Flexible/Adaptable				
Personally Credible				
Relationship builder				
Skilled Influencer				
Visionary				

149

6.   If your organisation had the time and funds to develop only one of the behavioural skills for the HR team this year, which one would you propose?

7.   Why do you consider the skill identified above as the most critical at this point in the organisation?

BEHAVIOURAL SKILLS DEVELOPMENT

8. What options are currently being utilized within your organisation for the development of HR Behavioural skills? Tick as many options as are applicable.

Options	Response
On the Job Exposure	
Executive Coaching	
Professional Body Membership	
External Training Programs	
Tailored Internal Training programs	
Short Term Assignments to another function	
Formal Mentoring Program	
Job Rotation Programs	
Participation in Communities of Practice	
Scheduled Experience Sharing Sessions	
Online experiential training programs	
Webinars	
Targeted CEO Coaching Sessions	
360 degree feedback programs	
Membership to key committees	

9. From your experience, what do you consider to be the most effective method for developing any behavioural skill (to change behaviour)?

    ....
    ....
    ....
    ....

10. What makes the development option identified above exceptionally effective?

    ....
    ....
    ....
    ....

BIBLIOGRAPHY

[1] Aitchison, D. (2007). "HR Transformation: Myth or Reality". HROA Europe and Sharedpertise Forums in Association with TPI. Survey Report, January 2007

[2] Allgeier, Sandy (2009). The Personal Credibility Factor: How to get it, Keep it and get it back (if you've lost it). Pearson Education Inc, New Jersey

[3] Armstrong, David (2006). Human Resource Management Practice. London: Kogan Page

[4] Birchfield, Reg (2003). "HR Management: The future of HR, what are the critical issues?" New Zealand Mangement

[5] Boselie, P. & Paauwe, J. (2004). "Human resource function competencies in European Companies". Personnel Review Vol. 34 No. 5, 2005 pp. 550-556

[6] Cheese, Peter; Thomas, J. Robert; Craig, Elizabeth (2008). The talent powered organisation: strategies for globalization, talent management and high performance. London: Kogan Page.

[7] CIPD (2009). "CIPD HR Professional Map".
     www.cipd.co.uk

[8] CIPD (2010). "Competency and competency frameworks".
     www.cipd.co.uk

[9] Covey, Stephen M. R & Merrill, Rebecca R. (2006). The
     Speed of Trust: the one thing that changes everything. Free
     Press, New York

[10] Ehlrich, C.J. (1997). "Human Resource Management: A
     changing script for a changing world". Human Resource
     Management. Volume 36; Issue 1 pg 85-90

[11] Grossman, J. Robert (2007). "New Competencies for HR:
     Researchers have Updated the Portfolio of Competencies
     for High Performing HR Professionals". HR Magazine:
     Society for Human Resource Management

[12] Lawler, E. E. & Mohrman, A. M. (2003). Creating a strategic
     human resource organisation: An assessment of trends and
     new directions. Stanford, CA: Stanford University Press.

[13] Lawler, E. Edward; Boundreau, W. John; Mohrman, Albers
     Susan; Mark, Tee Alice; Neilson, Beth; Osganian, Nora
     (2006). Achieving Strategic Excellence: Assessment of
     Human Resource Organisations. Stanford Business Press:
     Stanford, California

[14] Lengnick-Hall, L. Mark; Lengnick-Hall, A. Cynthia; Andrade,
     S. Leticia; Drake, Brian (2009). "Strategic human resource
     management: The evolution of the field". Human Resource
     Management Review 19, pg. 64-85

[15] Leon, Keith; Leon, Maura (2005). The Seven Steps to Successful Relationships (a practical guide for everyone). Babypie Publishing. Los Angeles, California

[16] Maxwell, John C. (2003) Leadership 101: What every leader needs to know. New York, Thomas Nelson Publishers

[17] Meisenger, R. Susan (2005) "The 4Cs of the HR profession: Being Competent, Curious, Courageous and Caring about People" in Losey, Michael; Meisenger, Sue; Ulrich, Dave (eds). The future of human resource management: 64 thought leaders explore the HR issues of today and tomorrow. New Jersey, John Willey & Sons Inc

[18] McCormick Nick (2007). Lead Well and Prosper: 15 Successful strategies for becoming a good boss. Be Good Publishing, New York

[19] Orme, Jackie (2009). A route map for the HR profession, People Management Magazine pg 16

[20] Oxfam GB (2005). "Developing HR Competencies" Guide

[21] Patterson, Kerry; Grenny, Joseph; Maxfield, David; McMillan, Ron; Switzler, Al (2008). Influencer: The power to change anything. New York, McGraw-Hill

[22] Perkins, P.S.; Brown, Les (2008) The Art and Science of Communication: Tools for Effective Communication in the Workplace. John Wikey & Sons Inc., Hoboken: New Jersey

[23] Pomeroy, Ann (2006). "The ethics squeeze: when business and ethics collide, HR is often caught in the middle". Human Resource Magazine

[24] Sparrow, Paul & Marchington, Mick (1998). Human Resource Management: The New Agenda. Pearson Education, London

[25] Stearns, Maureen (2004). Conscious Courage: Turning every day Challenges into Opportunities. Enrichment Books, Florida USA

[26] Steinhouse, Robbie (2010). Brilliant Decision Making: what the best decision makers know, do and say. London, Prentice Hall

[27] Torrington, Derek (1998) "Crisis and Opportunity in HRM: The Challenge for the Personnel Function" in Sparrow, Paul; Marchington, Mick. Human Resource Management: The New Agenda. Pearson Education, London.

[28] Ulrich, Dave; Brockbank, Wayne; Johnson, Dani (2008) HR Competencies: Mastery at the Intersection of People and Business. Society for Human Resources

[29] Ursiny, Tim (2005). The Confidence Plan: How to Build a Stronger You. Source Books, Inc; Napperville: Illinois.

[30] Vickers, Mark (2007) "HR growing pains: getting from awkward to accomplished" Human Resource Planning

[31] Wolosky, W. Howard (2008). "Closing the soft skills gap: the focus is in making soft skills part of the firm's psyche". The Practical Accountant, SourceMedia Inc.

[32] Zenger, John & Folkman, Joseph (2002). The Extraordinary Leader: Turning good managers into great leaders. Newyork: Mc Graw Hill